SPARKLY GREEN EARRINGS

Sparkly Green Earrings

Catching the light at every turn

– a memoir –

Melanie Shankle

Tyndale House Publishers, Inc.
Carol Stream, Illinois

Visit Tyndale online at www.tyndale.com.

Visit the author's blog at thebigmamablog.com.

TYNDALE and Tyndale's quill logo are registered trademarks of Tyndale House Publishers, Inc.

Sparkly Green Earrings: Catching the Light at Every Turn

Copyright © 2013 by Melanie Shankle. All rights reserved.

Cover image and script copyright © by Tyndale House Publishers, Inc. All rights reserved.

Author photo taken by Catherine Hornberger of Peacock Photography, copyright 2011. All rights reserved.

Designed by Jennifer Ghionzoli

Edited by Stephanie Rische

Published in association with William K. Jensen Literary Agency, 119 Bampton Court, Eugene, Oregon 97404.

Scripture taken from the Holy Bible, *New International Version,*® *NIV.*® Copyright © 1973, 1978, 1984, 2011 by Biblica, Inc.™ Used by permission of Zondervan. All rights reserved worldwide. www.zondervan.com.

Library of Congress Cataloging-in-Publication Data

Shankle, Melanie.
 Sparkly green earrings : catching the light at every turn / Melanie Shankle.
  p. cm.
 ISBN 978-1-4143-7171-9 (sc)
 1. Shankle, Melanie. 2. Motherhood—United States. 3. Motherhood—Religious aspects—
Christianity. I. Title.
 HQ759.S46153 2013
 306.874'30973—dc23   2012030434

Printed in the United States of America

19   18   17   16   15   14   13
7   6   5   4   3   2   1

TO CAROLINE:

If it weren't for you, this book wouldn't exist.

You are the absolute light of my life.

You have brought me joy, laughter,

and more happiness than you'll ever know.

You'll always be my best girl.

Contents

The Book of Dreams

OKAY. Y'ALL. APPARENTLY the hardest part of writing a book is figuring out where to begin. It's certainly not that I haven't always wanted to write a book, because I have. I've wanted to write a book ever since I read *Starring Sally J. Freedman as Herself* by Judy Blume in the fifth grade. Say what you want about *Are You There God? It's Me, Margaret*, but I have always been partial to Sally J.

And so my love of the written word compelled me to start a blog almost five years ago, when my daughter, Caroline, was not quite three years old. I knew I should document her childhood, and I also knew there was no way that was going to happen in any sort of scrapbook form unless I paid someone to do it for me because all those different papers and scissors and stickers totally freak me out. I have way too many perfectionistic tendencies to take on something that requires all that cutting and pasting.

In a shortsighted turn of events, I christened the blog Big Mama. I say shortsighted because there are now times when I'm out in public and someone will recognize me and call out, "BIG MAMA!" And then everyone in Starbucks will turn around to see if Martin Lawrence is there.

But the name Big Mama seemed appropriate at the time because that's what Caroline called me in those days. We were in that mode of getting rid of the pacifier my mother-in-law said she never should have had in the first place and learning to use the potty like a BIG GIRL, and Caroline decided there was no higher compliment that could be given than BIG. And so I became Big Mama.

Just like I'd always dreamed.

And that's the thing about motherhood. It's not like anything you imagine when you're eight years old and playing with your baby dolls and dreaming of the day you will have five children and name them Candy, Andy, Randy, Sandy, and Mandy. Or was that just me?

Why did I think it was a good idea to have children with rhyming names? More important, why did I think I'd ever survive five children? Probably because my only experience involved dressing up plastic dolls with synthetic hair that never talked back or had the kind of explosive diarrhea that ruined six outfits in four hours. Except that one time Baby Alive pooped a big piece of mold on me.

Real motherhood is different. It's better and it's messier and it's more complicated. It will break your heart and make you laugh harder than you ever imagined. You find yourself alternating between feeling like your friends talked you into some sort of pyramid scheme so you could share in their misery and thinking this is the most fulfilling thing you've ever done in your life.

And it makes you realize that if you really love your children, then you probably shouldn't give them all names that rhyme.

✳

The other night, long after I'd tucked Caroline into bed, I went back into her room to check on her and, truthfully, to watch her sleep. I'll never get tired of seeing the way she curls her hand up by her face and the way her lips relax and the way her long eyelashes rest on her cheeks while she sleeps. Not to mention it's one of the few times in the day when she's not arguing with me about the color of the sky or asking me to help her dig a hole in the backyard.

Lying next to her was a stack of papers filled with her drawings. There was a page entitled "Clothes I Want to Wear," complete with illustrations. From all appearances it looks like she has big plans to don a lot of muumuus with giant shoes. I've always wanted a daughter with ambitions to dress like a modern-day Mrs. Roper from *Three's Company*. And there was a page called "Places I Want to Live," with the subtitle "Beverly Hills." The accompanying sketch featured her walking down a palm-tree-lined sidewalk with a Chihuahua. I hold Jamie Lee Curtis and a cast of Prada-wearing, talking dogs directly responsible for that dream.

As I looked through all the pages, I appreciated the insight it gave me into her little mind. Sometimes the days get so busy that I miss these things. Then, as I stacked the papers to put them on her nightstand, I saw a title page that read, "Caroline's Book of Dreams."

There's no way she can know that some of the best dreams

she'll live are the ones she can't even imagine right now. The dreams that God has planted in her heart that she hasn't uncovered yet. Even though wearing a muumuu and walking a Chihuahua in Beverly Hills aren't necessarily bad ambitions.

Over the years, people began to tell me I should write a book. And I really wanted to. Except for the whole part that actually required me to sit down and write. But then I decided, how could eleven people and my dad be wrong?

So I'm writing this book. This is my Book of Dreams. The ones that came true and the ones that didn't, the ones that make me laugh and the ones that make me cry. Almost none of them involve wearing a muumuu, but all of them involve being a mother.

CHAPTER 1

Death, Taxes, & Motherhood

I ALWAYS ASSUMED I'd have a child someday. Like death and taxes and Barbara Walters, it seemed like an inevitable part of life. But I can't remember the exact moment Perry and I decided it was time for us to bring our own little person into the world.

However, I can guarantee we didn't put nearly as much thought into it as we probably should have. I mean, it's a person we're talking about. We were making the decision to create and then raise a human being. Which is much different than a dog, despite all those well-meaning people who compare their experience of raising a puppy to having a baby.

And, by the way, I was that person. It makes me want to go back in time and gouge out my own eyes when I think of how many times I compared my best friend Gulley's stories of sleepless nights with her newborn son to my own harrowing tales of getting out of bed to let our puppy, Scout, outside to go to the bathroom.

Yes, that's the same.

Idiot.

I think Perry and I both had the same perception of parenthood—something along the lines of "How hard can this be? After all, we've raised a puppy." Which is probably the same thing Cujo's owner thought. And we all know how that turned out.

But if I really think hard (which is something I try not to do very often), I'd say the whole baby thing began as Perry and I drove home from a beach vacation one day in June 2001. We'd just spent three glorious days at the beach, fishing and reading and doing whatever other relaxing pastimes we used to do prior to becoming parents. I'd give you all the details, but this isn't that kind of book.

We had the windows down and the Beastie Boys turned up loud. (Don't judge. Beach vacations mean the Beastie Boys to me. It's who I am. A child of the eighties. You've got to fight for your right to party.) We were a couple of tanned, relaxed fools listening to bad rap music.

Then my cell phone rang. I turned down the music and flipped open my phone. Because this was back in the days of yore when phones still flipped open and were incapable of telling you how well you slept the night before or what you needed to buy at the grocery store or how many steps you took that day.

(I read somewhere about a guy whose wife whispered, "Mark of the beast, mark of the beast," every time he used his iPhone to get directions and it was able to pinpoint his exact location.)

(Don't think about that too long or it will freak you out.)

Anyway, I opened my phone, and Gulley greeted me with, "I'm pregnant!"

Immediately I felt tears sting my eyes. My heart did some kind of weird flip that on second thought may have actually been my arteries hardening up, courtesy of my steady vacation diet of various forms of processed snack foods.

I wasn't shocked to hear she was pregnant. After all, I'd been with her the week before and watched her devour an entire plate of triple-cheese enchiladas, which totally aroused my suspicions. That day she'd said it was too soon to know for sure if she was pregnant but admitted it was a possibility.

Three-cheese enchiladas plus a bowl of queso seemed to indicate there was a good chance a baby was looking for some calcium to build strong bones and some fat to build chubby, edible baby thighs.

I was right. She was pregnant, and I couldn't have been happier for her. But in my happiness there was this twinge of loneliness or sadness or some other emotion that I couldn't nail down. I mean, this was Gulley. My very best friend in the entire world. The person I'd shared a ten-by-ten room with all during college. The person who has loved me through all my ups and downs, who has seen me laugh the hardest and cry the most and encouraged me in everything from my faith in God to getting my bangs cut. The person who has known me since we believed there was no finer outfit in the world than a pair of plaid walking shorts with a denim shirt and some loafers. Worn with socks.

We've been together since the days we'd nail a beach towel over the window so we could nap all day before going out all night. College: it really is where idiots are born. Or at least where they thrive.

Now I was afraid she was moving on to exciting new things without me. We'd managed to get married within a month of each other. Probably because God knew we'd each need the other one to talk about all the things we didn't know about marriage, such as HUSBANDS EXPECT DINNER. But now she was headed toward full-on adulthood in the form of becoming someone's mother. She was moving on to things like wearing jeans that went all the way past her belly button and discussing the merits of different types of fruit snacks for school lunches.

(Considering that was my perception of motherhood, it should come as no surprise that it took me five years of marriage to even consider it.)

(Having a dog doesn't require any of those things.)

(Although Scout will eat a fruit snack, if the opportunity arises.)

I hung up my phone, looked at Perry, and announced, "Gulley's pregnant." He took his eyes off the road and glanced over at me, and I watched the color drain from his face. "You want one, don't you?" he said.

"I don't know. I haven't really thought about it. Maybe. I don't know," I answered. Which was all a total lie. The truth was I had thought about it. I'd thought about it a lot, and I knew I wanted a baby. Most likely a bunch of them. I may have even had a list of baby names prepared. I was ready to move on to the next phase in our lives.

My eyes must have conveyed my real answer because all of a

sudden he said, "I feel like I'm going to throw up. I may need to pull over and throw up."

What can I say? I married romance.

It's safe to assume that the last hour of our trip was much quieter than the previous stretch as we tried to ignore the enormous elephant that had just dropped between us onto the console of the car.

For the next few months we engaged in the occasional conversation about having babies and listed all the pros and cons—and then September 11 happened, and it seemed like a bad time to bring a baby into the world. Especially because Perry went into some kind of mode like he was a contestant on *Survivor* and we had to do things like stockpile bottled water and cans of Vienna sausages in our garage. Although, let's be honest—I would rather die in some apocalyptic event than eat meat that comes from a can.

✳

And then came the day in January when I drove to Austin to be with Gulley while she delivered the most beautiful red-haired baby boy I'd ever seen. It didn't matter that her epidural didn't work the way it was supposed to or that I heard her actually growl when her husband had the poor judgment to enjoy a stick of beef jerky while she worked through a contraction. All that mattered was the barrel-chested, impossibly pink little boy in the nursery who made all the other babies seem sickly by comparison. All I could think was, *HOW CAN I GET ME ONE OF THOSE?*

But in spite of my fever for the babies, I knew we'd need to wait a little longer because we'd already committed to chaperone more than a hundred high school students on a spring break ski trip, and then we had plans to travel to Sicily with my parents so I could see the land of my ancestors. These are what you call first-world problems. Oh, we can't have a baby right now because we have to go to Colorado and ski and then go to Italy to tour Saint Peter's Basilica.

Looking back, I think the funniest part of all this is that we were under the illusion we were in control. That a baby would happen on our timetable, like we were a couple of fertile magicians pulling a rabbit out of a hat.

As it turned out, that wasn't exactly what God had planned for us. Yes, we would become parents (otherwise this would be a short book), but our path to getting there was harder and filled with more heartache than we'd counted on. I guess in a way it became our first lesson in the realities of parenthood. Which is to say, it can make you feel like a monkey in a windstorm.

CHAPTER 2

Eight Pregnancy
Tests Later . . .

ONE DAY IN April 2002 I began to suspect I might be pregnant. I wish I could tell you the exact day, but I've never been very good at math. I'm not sure how I knew precisely, because the symptoms were very similar to PMS: irritability, bouts of crying, and the occasional urge to throw a toaster oven through the kitchen window. But then came a morning when I tried to eat my standard breakfast of champions—Diet Coke with a side of Cocoa Puffs—and immediately felt like I needed to stick my entire head in the toilet.

I can't imagine why a baby would reject a breakfast chock-full of caffeine and synthetic chocolate puffs of sugar.

With trembling hands, I grabbed my car keys and headed to the closest drugstore to buy a six-pack of pregnancy tests, because I knew myself well enough to be sure I'd never believe the first five. I am obsessive and have a tendency to over-compensate in all areas, so there was no reason pregnancy should be any different.

The minute I got home, I ran to the bathroom to take the first test. Never mind that the instructions suggested it was best to use your first urine of the day.

(Of course, I've always had a notoriously small bladder, so how would I ever know if my first urine of the day was when I got up to go to the bathroom at 1 a.m. or 3 a.m. or 6 a.m.?)

(I'm not kidding. In college I used to drive Gulley crazy because I would go to the bathroom three times in about a ten-minute span before bed in the hope that my body would forgo the 3 a.m. bathroom wake-up call.)

(It never worked.)

Anyway, I tore open the test, figured out which end I was supposed to pee on, and then waited for the results. Within two minutes there was a very distinct double pink line indicating that I was, in fact, knocked up. And my first thought was, *Oh my word, I am pregnant.* Followed immediately by my second thought, which was, *Oh my word, I am pregnant.*

And then I thought of that old joke about the difference between a pregnant woman and a lightbulb.

(I'm sorry. But it's true.)

As I sat on the couch and waited for Perry to walk through the door, I felt an overwhelming sense of gratitude combined with a little anxiety. I thanked God for this new little life growing inside me and prayed that I wouldn't mess it up. A baby. We were going to have a baby. And it had happened so fast. I never even got to use the little ovulating indicator kit I'd bought at the drugstore for $14.99. I guess my mom had been right all those times she'd warned me it only takes ONE TIME to get pregnant.

Perry walked in a little while later and didn't even have a chance to shut the back door before I jumped on him and yelled, "I'M PREGNANT!" We hugged, we cried, we called everyone we knew to tell them the news, as if we were the first people on earth who had ever conceived a child. It was like we'd invented fire. Or something equally significant, like a chain of coffeehouses poised for world domination.

Several days later I went to the doctor's office to get my blood drawn to confirm that the eight pregnancy tests I'd taken were accurate. Yes, I said eight. I'd purchased two more in addition to the original six because you can never be too sure. What if the seven prior tests were all defective?

When I reached the eight-week mark, the doctor had me come in for an initial ultrasound, where they used something that looked like a curling iron gone wrong. Perry went with me, and we immediately saw a little bean with a beating heart on the screen. Dr. Hedges said everything looked good but asked us to come back the following week for a follow-up ultrasound just to make sure everything was okay.

And here's where I have to admit it never occurred to me that something might be wrong. I just thought this was standard procedure or maybe he really liked us and wanted to give us the chance to see our baby again because we were so excited. I think, based on this information, it's safe to say I'm an optimist at heart.

A week later we were back at the doctor's office while he

scanned the screen to find our baby. And then he scanned some more. And then some more. Perry held one of my hands, and suddenly I realized Dr. Hedges was taking my other hand. He looked at me with sad eyes and said, "I'm sorry. The baby is gone. There isn't a heartbeat."

Well, that was not what I was expecting to hear.

Heartbroken, I looked up at Perry and realized he'd turned completely white. The doctor noticed it too because he immediately pressed the intercom button and called for a nurse to help with "a big oak" that was about to go down. I will always remember that moment because even in the sadness, I thought it was odd that he'd just referred to my husband as a big oak.

I sat there feeling numb and exposed, desperately wishing I was wearing more than a thin, backless hospital gown as Dr. Hedges began to talk to us about scheduling a D and C procedure and hospital check-in times and other logistics to remove this baby, our baby, who was no longer alive.

All of a sudden I felt as if I couldn't breathe. The reality started to fall in on me as I got dressed and walked through the waiting room full of pregnant women. I'd just been one of those smiling pregnant women a few minutes before. Now, in the span of one short ultrasound, I was fighting back tears and holding a slip of paper with a hospital appointment time. The grief settled in my chest, and I wanted to run away. But where do you go when the pain is coming from somewhere inside you?

Perry and I walked robotically to the car with such a sense of loss over something we'd just now realized we wanted so much. Our baby was gone. Slowly, I picked up my cell phone and started making the hardest calls I'd ever made in my life.

There was no easy way to tell our parents and close friends that we'd lost the baby, but I wanted to get it over with. My strategy was to face the pain head-on and put it behind us as soon as possible. Which is great, except pain doesn't really work that way. It's sneaky. It hits you in the middle of the night when things are quiet, and it whispers that it may never go away. As soon as I got my daddy on the phone and told him our news, the dam broke. The tears fell like they'd never stop, and my shoulders began to shake in that way they do when you're headed straight for an ugly cry. This was going to be the first grandchild, and I felt like we'd let everybody down.

We were hit with the sobering reality that this whole parenting gig might be a little harder than we'd originally thought back when we believed the most difficult part would be deciding on a name the kids on the playground couldn't turn into an insult.

CHAPTER 3

The Worst Summer Ever

LIKE MOST THINGS in life, the miscarriage ended up being a lot more complicated than I'd originally thought. Perry and I were sad, but we figured we'd try again in a month or so. I went back for a routine follow-up visit to the doctor, and they had me take a pregnancy test to confirm everything had gone as planned with the D and C.

The doctor didn't seem concerned when the test came back positive. He just told me to wait one more week, take a test at home, and call his office if it came back positive. Which is exactly what happened. I was instructed to come in for a blood test so they could get a better reading on my hormone levels and try to figure out what was going on with my body.

I was in Dallas on a business trip, trying to function like a normal person, not someone who wanted to stay in bed forever curled up from the sadness, when my doctor called me. (The doctor called me personally on my cell phone. Not his nurse. Not a staff member. The doctor. This couldn't bode well.)

He explained that there were some complications, and he used words like *molar pregnancy*, *tumor*, and *cancer*. Apparently my body didn't realize I was no longer pregnant, and rogue cells had begun to congregate in my uterus like a band of terrorists plotting some sort of jihad. The conversation ended with his advice to "go home immediately."

This probably goes without saying, but I began to cry and couldn't stop. I cried as I explained to my manager that I needed to get on the first flight out of Dallas, I cried when I called Perry to explain what was going on, and I cried until I hyperventilated when I talked to my daddy and heard the concern in his voice.

I boarded my flight home to San Antonio and have no doubt I was one of those people who fellow passengers are deeply concerned about but are a little afraid to talk to lest they become emotionally unhinged.

Perry picked me up from the airport, and I almost collapsed with relief when I saw him. He is always the voice of reason, the one who will balance my outstanding ability to go right to the worst-case scenario and set up a tent to camp there indefinitely. As I blurted out all the what-ifs and whys, he remained steady and reminded me that God was in control and we'd know more after our doctor's appointment the next morning.

As I lay in bed that night, after we'd asked God for wisdom and peace, I felt the fear and anxiety start to settle in again. But then I heard the voice of God as close to audible as anything

I'd ever experienced: "It doesn't matter what the doctors say. It only matters what I say. I am in control."

Peace washed over me, and I had a deep sense that everything was going to be okay, even if we were on a different road than I'd planned.

The next morning I opened my Bible to Isaiah 55 and felt these words jump off the page:

> You will go out in joy
>   and be led forth in peace;
> the mountains and hills
>   will burst into song before you,
> and all the trees of the field
>   will clap their hands.
>
> ISAIAH 55:12

It felt like God's promise to me that I would be brought back to a place of joy at some point in the future even if I couldn't imagine it at the moment. And I held on to that promise with complete desperation.

When we got the doctor's report, it turned out that I hadn't had a normal miscarriage—I'd had the deluxe version, thanks to a partial molar pregnancy. A version that required me to get my blood drawn every week to check hormone levels and do a bunch of other medical-jargon things that went over my head because all I wanted to know was, *When can I have a baby?*

Perry and I refer to this time as The Worst Summer Ever.

I wish I could say I spent this entire postmiscarriage season filled with peace, but that would be a lie. There are only so many times you can get stuck with a needle by an unsympathetic nurse and not get angry. Not to mention my hormone levels weren't dropping like they were supposed to and my arms were beginning to have track marks, thanks to the aggressive blood draws. I knew I was in trouble when I cried during an old episode of *Sanford and Son*. Of course, the bigger question may be why I was watching this antiquated television show about a junk dealer and his son in the first place. I was in a dark hole.

By September things still weren't going as planned. I was told that I'd need to have powerful injections of some drug with a name that had a disproportionate number of consonants in it, and because of that drug, I'd need to wait three more months before I could try to get pregnant again.

Yet only two months later, I felt pretty sure Perry and I might be poor candidates for any sort of "safe sex" campaign. I drove to the store to load up on pregnancy tests, and it took exactly five minutes to confirm that, yes, I was pregnant. Again. Ahead of schedule. And pretty confused about how exactly this had transpired. In fact, when I went to see my doctor the following week, I apologized, explaining, "I'm not sure how this happened."

He offered to buy me a book about the whole process.

I think he was being sarcastic.

So it all began again. Except this time I knew how fragile that little life inside me was, largely because I'd spent so much time on various pregnancy message boards on the Internet, which made it seem like the rarest exception of all when babies actually make it. I mean, have you read *What to Expect When You're Expecting*? As if I couldn't make up enough worst-case scenarios all by myself, now I was worrying about things I'd never even considered, like toxoplasmosis. Which apparently is some kind of blood infection you can get from a cat. And I didn't even own a cat. I'd thought about owning a cat, though, and what if that counted?

But at some point I realized I could spend this entire pregnancy in complete fear and paranoia about cats and other potential issues, or I could let go and trust that God was in control of this little person I was growing from scratch. I realize that technically it's not from scratch so much as the merging of a sperm and an egg, but that's pretty darn close to making something from nothing. You're welcome for that free reproductive lesson.

All I knew was that if this pregnancy was going to result in a real, live, human baby I would raise to adulthood, I didn't want to look back and regret that I'd spent the entire nine months living in fear and dread about what might happen. I wanted to embrace all the mornings I spent with my head in a toilet and the midnight runs for six or eleven glazed donuts . . . for the baby. I wanted to look at books filled with baby names and throw out my suggestions to Perry while he sat on the couch and watched hunting shows starring Ted Nugent and tell him, "No way are we naming this baby Ted. Or Nugent."

The only guarantee I had was that God was in control. He was the one who knew the plans he had for me and this little baby and our family. And while I didn't even pretend to understand his ways and still felt a little raw from the miscarriage and the heartbreak of the previous summer, I trusted him with the outcome. So I sat back and prepared to enjoy my pregnancy and prayed that God would bless us with a baby who would grow into a strong, fearless leader with a lot of personality.

He hasn't always answered my prayers in the ways I've expected—in fact, most of the time he answers in ways I never could have thought up. But, man, I think that time he was in heaven thinking, *Just you wait.* Because we got all those things and then some.

Now we're just holding on for the ride.

CHAPTER 4

In the Ghetto

GROWING UP IN Sunday school, I always heard that God gives everyone special gifts. Some people can sing like angels, others have the gift of encouragement, and a lucky few can get on the dance floor and dance in such a way that people will form a circle around them just to watch.

Not one of those things is my gift. Even though there were times in college when I drank enough Zima to fancy myself quite the dancer.

As for me, I possess the unique talent of making stressful situations even more tense by taking on more than any person with such limited organizational skills and a short attention span should. (Look! Something shiny!) This may explain why I convinced Perry it was a good idea for us to completely renovate our home during my pregnancy.

Actually, we'd decided to start the project months earlier, and I didn't really see a reason to postpone it just because I was having a baby. So we loaded up our truck and we moved to Beverly. (Hills, that is. Swimming pools, movie stars . . .)

Except it wasn't nearly as glamorous, nor were we nearly as sophisticated and prepared as the Clampetts. And it wasn't Beverly Hills. Even so, we packed up our entire house and moved into a rental home a few miles away while we began a construction project that still remains the strongest evidence that our marriage will last forever. Because if we survived that, we can survive anything.

There's so much talk about the divorce rate in the United States, but I think all that could change if one of the requirements for getting a marriage license is that the couple must first complete some sort of home renovation project together. All those trips to Home Depot, the debates about budgets, decisions about paint colors, and the day your beloved tells you there will be no granite countertops—those are the tests of true love. That's when you know if this is someone you want to be with for the long haul—or when you realize you're already stuck with that person for a lifetime. A lifetime spent with laminate countertops instead of granite. But really, I'm over it.

As for us, we took on this enormous construction project long after we'd said our vows and while I was simultaneously spending my days at Babies "R" Us obsessing over all the different bottle options and trying to determine whether a wipe warmer was something you actually needed in order to have a baby.

(You don't, by the way. That baby will be high maintenance enough without creating the expectation for a warm wet wipe.)

And when I say that we took on the construction project, I mean that Perry contracted the entire job and worked tirelessly to make sure everything turned out the way we wanted while I cried every night because I was worried the house wouldn't be ready on time and, oh my word, what if we had to bring our new baby girl home to a rental house instead of her new pink nursery?

I'd like to blame pregnancy hormones for my constant obsession over when the house would be finished, but I know I'd act the same way tomorrow except I wouldn't be able to sing a chorus of "In the Ghetto" by Elvis Presley to drive home my point because the words "a poor little baby child is born—in the ghetto" wouldn't have the same impact now that the baby is eight years old.

I even climbed on scaffolding to help hang crown molding when I was eight months pregnant in my desperation to get the house finished. I realize this doesn't trump Mary having to ride to Bethlehem on a donkey and give birth in a stable, but it feels like a close second.

$$*$$

We moved back into the house exactly two weeks before Caroline was born, in spite of the fact that we had no kitchen counter-tops or other necessary components that make up a kitchen. But we had the pink nursery, and that's all that really mattered. Who needs an oven when you have darling, whimsical letters that spell *CAROLINE* hanging on a pink wall and a fresh, white crib that the baby won't actually sleep in for several months?

Along the way there were high points and low points. And

then there was Joe, the guy we hired to tile our shower, who had never actually installed tile.

Joe tiled the shower stall in our new master bathroom. We originally hired a man named Mr. Baldo of Baldo and Son Construction to work on the shower and other various jobs, but Mr. Baldo took off with our money before he ever completed all the work we'd hired him to do.

Of course, we shouldn't have been shocked by this turn of events, considering he'd already admitted to us that he didn't actually have a son, even though his business was named Baldo and Son. I guess he just felt that the "and Son" gave him an air of legitimacy, much like Fred Sanford.

Two months before my due date, we found ourselves without a tile guy and with a shower that desperately needed to be tiled. And it's a fact of life that at the intersection of crazy and desperate, you'll find lowered standards. One of our subcontractors mentioned that his brother-in-law, Joe, might be available to do some tile work, so we called him. He was more than happy to take the job, his price was reasonable, and best of all, he could start the next day.

Joe showed up promptly the next morning with his bucket of grout and began laying tile in the shower. He turned out to be quite the conversationalist, and while he was working, he began to chat extensively with Perry. They talked about the neighborhood and our construction project, and then Joe said, "You know what, Mr. Perry? I didn't even know how to install tile until last week, but I bought a video at Home Depot, and now I think I know what I'm doing."

Well.

That certainly is comforting, Joe.

You'd think he might have kept that bit of information to himself, but I guess Joe was a firm believer in being transparent. We soon discovered he was a firm believer in something else too.

Perry returned to the job site one morning and could tell Joe had left in a hurry. His tools were strewn about the bathroom, and he hadn't covered the bucket of grout. When Joe showed up that day, Perry asked him what had happened. Joe informed him our house was haunted and we needed to have some sort of exorcism.

Okay, sure. Let's get that scheduled. What are your thoughts on a nice housewarming party combined with an exorcism? Will people bring gifts? Perhaps a nice mango-scented candle and some holy oil?

When pressed further, Joe based his suspicion on hearing voices after everyone else had left. Never mind the fact that every window in the house was left open and we lived in a corner house where people were constantly walking by. The logical conclusion, according to Joe, was that we had some ghosts. Obviously plural, because although I don't know much about ghosts, I bet they don't travel alone. They likely travel in packs, the way women visit the restroom when they're out together.

We never did have the house exorcised, and shockingly, we've never had any more ghost issues. However, there is something in our house that's extremely frightening: the tile job in our shower. It's painfully obvious we didn't need a priest as much as we needed someone with more tile experience than an hour-long tutorial from a Home Depot video.

After we moved back into the house, I attempted to clean the construction dirt and grime off the tile in the shower. I finally gave up, realizing it was impossible to get it completely clean thanks to all the jagged lines and grout imperfections. I griped about it regularly to Perry, questioning how anyone would be bold enough or dumb enough to take on a job with no experience other than watching a video.

But then it hit me. Was that really so different from what we were doing? Weren't we taking on the most monumental job in the world in deciding to have a child? And what did we know? We were just two dumb kids. Kids in our early thirties, but kids nonetheless. How else do you explain that most of our meals were cooked in the microwave and we considered donuts to be part of a balanced breakfast? I prided myself on the fact I'd read upward of two whole books on the parenting process, but in reality I could only wish for something as extensive as a Home Depot video production on how to be a parent.

Like Anne Lamott says in *Traveling Mercies*, "I always imagined when I was a kid that adults had some kind of inner toolbox full of shiny tools: the saw of discernment, the hammer of wisdom, the sandpaper of patience. But then when I grew up I found that life handed you these rusty bent old tools—friendships, prayer, conscience, honesty—and said, Do the best you can with these, they will have to do. And mostly, against all odds, they're enough."

Perry and I were going to walk this road, hoping for the advice of friends and parents and well-meaning old ladies at the grocery store to get us through, but most of all, knowing we were completely dependent on God to give us wisdom about how to lay all the tiles of childhood as straight as we could and to smooth in the grout with the hope of covering our own imperfections and making them work with the overall design and personality of our daughter.

Of course we couldn't have known then that we'd also have times, much like Joe, when we'd wonder if the creation we were working on might be possessed. Especially from ages two through four. But I'm getting ahead of myself.

CHAPTER 5

Shamu & the Chicken Spaghetti

ONE DAY SHORTLY after Joe the tile novice left us, I decided I might feel better and eliminate some stress if I took a day off from obsessing about the house and singing "In the Ghetto" to relax and get a little color on my very pregnant physique. Yes, because that would make it look better. Whenever I visit Sea World, I always hear people remark that Shamu would look a lot smaller if only he had a tan.

So in a flash of brilliance, I decided to put on a swimsuit and sit in the backyard to get some sun. And to maximize my efforts, I contorted my seven-months-pregnant body into a nonmaternity bikini, even though there was maximum spillage everywhere. Looking good. But I figured no one would see me, and really, in the long run, wouldn't a little bit of a tan make my pregnant body look so much better?

The answer was literally a big, fat no, but God bless me for my optimism. The only thing that was going to make me look better at that point was childbirth, accompanied by an ensuing maximum-weight-loss diet plan—oh, and the evaporation of the fifteen pounds of water I was retaining in my ankles.

I was in the middle of gathering my crucial laying-out-in-the-sun supplies, such as *InStyle* magazine, a bottle of water, and a towel, when the phone rang. As I was talking on the phone, I walked into the backyard without realizing I hadn't brought any of my things out with me. I turned to go back inside and realized I had shut, and therefore locked, the back door behind me.

I was standing in the backyard of our rental home, seven months pregnant, in a bikini swimsuit with no towel, no T-shirt, and no tarp to cover my large, exposed self. I immediately began weighing my options. I tried all the back windows. They were shut tight. I contemplated hoisting my pregnant body over the chain-link fence in the hope that the front door might be unlocked.

Now there is a mental image. A huge, pregnant woman in a too-small bikini climbing a chain-link fence. It's enough to make a person wish they didn't have eyes. Never mind that it would have taken a forklift or maybe even a crane to get me over that fence.

After I quit panicking, I realized I had a phone with me, so I called Perry on his cell phone and explained what had happened. After he quit laughing hysterically, he said that he'd get home as soon as he could. But he was about forty-five minutes away.

I spent those minutes talking on the phone to Gulley while intermittently drinking water out of the garden hose to keep myself hydrated and hanging out of an increasingly small swim-suit. It was a scene straight from an episode of *Cops*.

Perry finally arrived after what seemed like hours and saved his waddling damsel in distress. Air-conditioning and a mater-nity dress that actually covered my body had never felt so good. I know people always say pregnant women glow, but I think it's only because the pregnancy hormones make you so hot that you have no other choice but to walk around with sweat glistening on your face the majority of the time. Plus, I adamantly believe that people, especially husbands, are just a little frightened by pregnant women and their ability to completely freak out at a moment's notice, so they try to come up with verbs that have a positive connotation.

That day marked the end of my attempts to try to be beau-tiful and pregnant at the same time. Along with a lesson that perhaps I shouldn't be so vain. Maybe now that I was about to be someone's mother, I should worry more about things like researching the safest car seats and putting those plastic child-proof plugs in electrical sockets instead of lying out in the sun like I was still in college and skipping my biology lab. And certainly there would be plenty of time to lie out in the sun and relax after I had the baby. Right?

*

Our house was finally finished by the middle of July. Of course, *finished* is a relative term. It was inhabitable. As long as you don't consider a functioning kitchen to be an essential part of a home—and there are plenty of tribes in countries all over the world that don't. Personally, I always enjoy a legitimate reason to pick up Mexican food for dinner. Washing our dishes with the hose in the backyard was a little awkward, but that only lasted until Perry brought in a piece of plywood and a twenty-five-dollar temporary sink he bought at Home Depot.

I constantly complained about the lack of proper air-conditioning that summer. I would lie in bed next to Perry at night and launch into a six-part lecture, complete with bullet points, about how I couldn't believe we'd spent all this money on new air-conditioning units that didn't actually cool off our house. I felt certain we'd been a part of some elaborate air-conditioning con job and wrote numerous letters in my head to the Better Business Bureau about our shady heating and cooling company. Perry never really responded to my rants about how our bedroom felt like the surface of the sun. But that might have been because he was too wrapped up in three down comforters to hear me.

We spent the next few weeks unpacking all our things, hanging pictures, and getting splinters from our makeshift kitchen countertops. But all that really mattered to me was that I could sit in the pink rocker in the nursery at nighttime and pray for our new baby girl, who was about to make her big debut. God had given me a verse for her a few months earlier, and I'd sit in the silence of that freshly painted nursery and whisper the words like a prayer:

I will pour water on the thirsty land,
    and streams on the dry ground;
I will pour out my Spirit on your offspring,
    and my blessing on your descendants.

They will spring up like grass in a meadow,
> like poplar trees by flowing streams.
Some will say, "I belong to the LORD";
> others will call themselves by the name of Jacob;
still others will write on their hand, "The LORD's."

ISAIAH 44:3-5

Ultimately, as much as I hoped and prayed for a healthy, perfect baby, what I desired more than anything else was to raise a child who would know the joy of putting God first in her life and the wisdom as a parent to show her what that looks like. Perry had lost his dad in an accident when he was just nine years old, the same age I was when my parents divorced. I had a difficult relationship with my mother, and Perry couldn't fill a bucket with what he knew about girls. Both of us felt like we were venturing into uncharted territory here, and we knew we couldn't do this by ourselves. In fact, I think we knew at some level then, and we are continuing to learn more and more, that we're doing it *in spite of* ourselves. We are two very imperfect souls who have been entrusted with a little piece of heaven, and we don't take that lightly.

✳

The last week of July finally rolled around, and we got the call from the countertop people that they were ready to finish our kitchen. Perry scheduled them for Friday, August 1, and decided it would be a great opportunity for him to take a last-minute trip down to the national seashore to fish and camp out for the night. Because he was apparently trying to kill me.

Who thinks it's a good idea to leave your wife, who is currently nine months pregnant, to drive to a remote destination with no cell service to catch sharks? Other than someone who has a death wish. He agreed to wait to leave until after my doctor's appointment that Thursday morning. Probably because I'd spent the previous twenty-four hours informing him that missing the birth of your first child is the kind of thing a woman never gets over. NEVER. Like on my deathbed I would hold his hand and whisper, "Remember how you weren't there when our baby was born?"

But my doctor checked me out and said it didn't look like I was going into labor anytime soon. And with that proclamation, Perry packed up his fishing rods and his common sense and headed toward the coast. Meanwhile, I stayed home to supervise the kitchen crew as they installed everything, and I made plans with my mother-in-law for her to come over early Saturday morning to help me unpack boxes and organize the new kitchen.

Because God loves Perry, he came home safe and sound from his shark expedition late Friday afternoon. We had plans to attend a dinner party that night for our church, so I did the necessary acrobatics to get myself into the last of my maternity tops that still fit (and a pair of heels, which has no relevance to this story, but I was proud of myself for suffering for the sake of fashion and felt that you should know) and waddled out for our big night on the town. Or a big night eating chicken spaghetti and talking about future plans for our church. Same difference. Unless you are in your teens and envisioning how glamorous life will be someday.

We had a nice night and even had some friends come back to our house to get the official tour of the remodel. Finally, around midnight, Perry and I crawled into bed, and I commenced my nightly ritual of complaining about all the ways we'd been suckered into buying a subpar air-conditioning unit while Perry put on his stocking cap and wool socks.

Around 3:00 a.m. I woke up like someone had slapped me. I sat straight up and immediately knew something wasn't right. But then the feeling went away, and I lay down to go back to sleep. Twenty minutes later, just as I'd drifted off, I woke up again. And I knew. I knew. Clearly, I'd eaten some bad chicken spaghetti. There was no other explanation for the way my stomach was cramping. Certainly not the fact that I was nine and a half months pregnant and possibly in labor.

Bless my heart.

I continued to lie there in denial, fuming about the unsanitary nature of poultry in general and casseroles in particular, as I experienced wave after wave of food poisoning. Exactly twenty minutes apart. And then fifteen minutes apart. And then ten minutes apart.

Around 6:00 a.m. I finally began to come out of my haze of denial, shook Perry lightly, and said, "Hey. I think I might be in labor."

He rubbed the sleep out of his eyes. "Do I have time to take a shower?" he asked, scratching his head.

Really? Do you have time to take a shower? How am I supposed to know that? Until about thirty minutes ago, I thought I had food poisoning. I am an idiot.

I told him he probably had time to take a shower because

that was obviously the most pressing matter at hand. In the meantime, I called my parents, Gulley, and my sister to let them know I may or may not be, but probably was, in labor, but I could also be in the throes of a case of salmonella that hit with waves of astonishing regularity.

Then I called my mother-in-law, who was supposed to arrive in about an hour to help me with the kitchen. She asked, "So should I not come over?"

And I responded with an emphatic, "No, you need to come over right now and help me get this kitchen unpacked!"

Because in what can only be described as "labor logic," I felt like I could survive childbirth but I couldn't handle bringing my baby home to a house without an organized silverware drawer and Tupperware cabinet.

This was not the ghetto.

This was our home. And it was about to have a real, live baby in it.

CHAPTER 6

I Wanted My Epidural in the First Trimester

I THINK IT'S important for you to know that there was a time in my life when I seriously considered adopting any potential children I might have. Not out of any sense of compassionate obligation, but because I thought the best method of childbirth might be to completely skip the whole birth part of that equation and go straight to the precious little bundle wrapped up like a burrito.

There are women who want to experience natural childbirth, but those are probably the same women who run marathons. I am not one of those women. I believe in the miracles of modern medicine, and that includes epidurals. Which is why one of the first questions I asked my doctor upon finding out I was pregnant was "How soon can I get the meds?" When he encouraged me to write an official birth plan, mine was a single piece of paper with "EPIDURAL!!!!!" scrawled in large letters with a Sharpie pen.

Honestly, I longed for the good old days my grandmother told me about when a woman would go into the hospital to have a baby and wake up two days later with memories of vague hallucinations and a child in her arms. But apparently that option is no longer available, thanks to the marvel of medical advances.

And since I was so certain I wanted no part of any kind of natural childbirth pain, I didn't see the need for Perry and me to waste any time going to those free childbirth classes the hospital offers. Why would we do that when it was Trista's season on *The Bachelorette* and it looked like she might have a real shot at lasting love with Ryan, the cute fireman? (And, by the way, they're still together, so I think it's clear I made the right choice.) Not to mention I was spending all my free time catching up on every episode of *Alias*, and clearly Sydney Bristow and Vaughn and the takedown of SD-6 were way more important than learning how to breathe through the childbirth pains I was sure I wouldn't experience.

(There may have been a week when I seriously tried to convince Perry that we should name our child Sydney Bristow.)

(I also suggested the name Owen, for unknown reasons. But quickly scratched it off the list when I remembered we were having a girl. Plus Perry always said "Owen" like the Momma character in *Throw Momma from the Train*.)

The only thing I did to prepare for childbirth, other than fantasize about having arms that looked like Sydney Bristow's, was to take the official tour of the hospital. This is when I learned a critical piece of information: there is no guarantee that you get a private room after delivery. The nurse giving the tour to our little band of seven or eight expecting couples ended our tour by whispering in a confidential tone, "The best advice I can give you if it's really important for you to have your own room is to remember that the squeaky wheel gets the grease." And I vowed then and there to be the squeakiest wheel Methodist Hospital had ever seen.

✳

After a day of on-and-off contractions and furious unpacking of boxes, around 5:00 p.m. on Saturday, August 2, I finally called the doctor's answering service and told them I thought I was in labor. The on-call doctor returned my call, and I informed her that my contractions were about seven minutes apart. She agreed it was probably time for me to head to the hospital. Perry and I gathered our bags and my assortment of pillows and loaded them into the Ford Taurus that I'd insisted my brother-in-law, Chris, vacuum out for me earlier in the day because *I can't bring my baby home in a dirty car.*

(I was a joy to be around.)

(Kind of like a rabid cat. I may have even hissed.)

As Perry drove to the hospital, my contractions began to get stronger and harder. I might have said some words you'll never hear in Sunday school, unless you go to one of those churches that is trying SUPER hard to be relevant to today's culture. Perry began to pray for me as he was driving—that God would give the doctors and nurses wisdom, that it would be an easy delivery, that I would not be afraid. And then he looked at me and said, "This is the last time we're going to be alone for a long time."

It was his attempt at humor, a way to lighten the moment. But I sucked in my breath, looked at him, and burst into tears. I think it's times like this he wishes he'd followed his original life plan to live on a remote ranch and spend his days hunting and fishing all by himself. "What? What did I say?" he questioned.

"This is it," I replied. "We won't be alone again for eighteen years. At least. And our lives are about to totally change, and there is no going back."

He looked at me with a straight face and said, "Yes, it's called parenthood. We signed up for it nine months ago."

I knew that. But in that moment I felt overwhelmed by what was about to happen and how much our lives were about to be turned upside down. I was terrified of labor, in more pain than I'd expected from contractions, and desperately wishing I'd gone to at least one of those classes that would have taught me to breathe like "Hoo, hee, hoo" while focusing on a spot on the wall.

We drove around the hospital parking lot looking for a parking place and resisting the urge to yell out the window, "Hey, black Suburban, we're about to have a baby. I hope you need that parking spot more than we do."

After we finally parked and unloaded our stuff, we began to make our way to the hospital entrance, but I had to stop in the middle of the sidewalk because I was overcome by a contraction. All those episodes of *Alias* were not helpful in that moment.

Perry left our bags and hurried to get me into the hospital while I called out to anyone who appeared to be official hospital personnel, "I would like a private room, please! Can I get a private room?" The little candy striper in the elevator removed her arm from my death grip and whispered, "I'll see what I can do, ma'am, but I'm just a volunteer."

Eventually I made it to a room and was given a hospital gown to change into with instructions to get in the bed and wait for the nurse to come check me. I lay there as Perry held my hand, just knowing that the nurse would probably determine I was at least six centimeters dilated. How else could they explain the pain and frequency of these contractions?

Several minutes later Nurse Louise entered the room. And I immediately knew, the way you know when the milk has gone bad, that she didn't subscribe to the warm and fuzzy method of labor and delivery. She walked in, surveyed the room, and wrinkled her nose like she had just smelled weakness and it made her stomach turn. I tried to make polite small talk as she checked me for signs of labor, and I only half-jokingly asked, "So, when will the anesthesiologist be here?"

Nurse Louise looked at me suspiciously and replied, "You're only one centimeter dilated. I don't know if you're really even in labor, and you certainly don't need the anesthesiologist." Like I was some kind of drug-seeking patient who had come to the hospital looking to get an epidural for recreational use.

One centimeter dilated. Well, that was certainly disappointing. All that pain? All those contractions? For one lousy centimeter?

My sister, my mother-in-law, and Gulley had all followed us to the hospital, and once Nurse Louise declared that a birth wasn't imminent and it was possible I was faking the entire thing, they sent my brother-in-law to pick up McDonald's for dinner. They all began to have social hour while eating their cheeseburgers, and they placed bets on what time the baby would arrive. It was all fun and games until a major contraction hit me, and I may or may not have said in a forced tone, "I'm going to need you all to be quiet and take your french fries outside." I've never seen people jump so quickly to meet my french fry demands.

I spent the next several hours in increasing pain, hooked up to a monitor that clearly indicated I was having healthy contractions, yet Nurse Louise continued to insist I didn't need the epidural yet. Perry believed differently, especially after I wrenched his thumb out of its socket during one particularly intense moment.

Then the doctor on call came in—a very nice woman, I'm sure, but she wasn't aware of my master epidural plan. She was concerned that my labor wasn't progressing. (Really? Because it felt like progression. It felt like an alien was about to burst out of my stomach holding my intestines.) She also decided I was measuring small for a full-term pregnancy, so she sent me off to have an ultrasound.

As they wheeled me down the hall, I clutched Perry's hand like it was my personal lifeline, but they stopped at the door to the ultrasound room and said he couldn't go in with me. I was taken into a small, dark place with no one I loved around me, filled with worry and fear that something might be wrong with our baby girl. I lay on the hospital bed as the technician rubbed cold gel on my stomach, and the tears began to fall. It was all too much. This was way too hard. I don't know that I've ever felt so alone.

Then I heard a voice whisper in the darkness: "You're not alone. I'm here." And I began to quote what I remembered of Psalm 121 to myself:

> I lift up my eyes to the mountains—
>   where does my help come from?
> My help comes from the LORD,
>   the Maker of heaven and earth.
>
> He will not let your foot slip—
>   he who watches over you will not slumber;
> indeed, he who watches over Israel
>   will neither slumber nor sleep.
>
> The LORD watches over you—
>   the LORD is your shade at your right hand;
> the sun will not harm you by day,
>   nor the moon by night.
>
> The LORD will keep you from all harm—
>   he will watch over your life;
> the LORD will watch over your coming and going
>   both now and forevermore.

Peace began to wash over me, and I knew it was true: I wasn't alone. I didn't know if everything was going to be okay, but I knew with all certainty that Jesus was right there with me in that scary hospital room as the ultrasound technician moved the wand back and forth across my stomach.

I think there are times in life when he takes away all those earthly things we look to for comfort and security so we can feel him better and love him more. This was one of those moments for me. In my coming and going, he was with me.

CHAPTER 7

Straight from Heaven

THE DOCTOR MET Perry and me back in the labor and delivery room and announced that everything was okay and our baby girl appeared to be in the healthy seven- to eight-pound range. Then she left the room, and I didn't see her or Nurse Louise for a few hours while I continued to wonder what they had against epidurals and if they secretly hated me because I'd been so belligerent about the whole private room thing. Maybe the squeaky wheel gets the private room but not the epidural? Chalk that up to things I wish I'd known earlier.

As we found out much later, there was an emergency C-section in the next room with major complications. The hospital was short staffed because it was a Saturday night, and my "routine" labor got lost in the shuffle. When Nurse Louise finally showed up to check my progress around midnight, she got a stunned look on her face and immediately paged the doctor, who came in and announced I was fully dilated. They both acted shocked and surprised.

You know who wasn't surprised? Me. I'd been in so much pain in the last few hours that I couldn't believe women ever had sex again after one round of childbirth. I looked at Perry and hoped he'd be satisfied living the life of a monk because there was no way I was going to do anything to risk this kind of foolishness again.

Nothing in life had prepared me for this kind of pain. I realize this is extremely comforting for those of you who might be reading this while pregnant with your first child. But bear with me. It will be okay. Just make sure you yell for your epidural before you holler about getting a private room.

When the doctor told me I was ready to go, I wailed, "What about my epidural? I wanted the epidural. Please. Get. Me. The. Epidural." I may have growled that last part. She immediately paged the anesthesiologist, and I was so relieved I hadn't missed the "epidural window" I'd heard so much about that I began to sob.

A few minutes later my knight in shining armor came sweeping through the door with a tray of bliss. As he scrubbed my back and helped me sit up on the table, I whispered, "I've never loved anyone more." And at that moment I absolutely meant it. Forget Perry. He was the one who'd gotten me into this mess in the first place.

The medicine began to take effect, and I came back to my real self, as evidenced by the fact I called for someone to bring me my lip gloss TOOT SUITE and told everyone to gather around me for a group picture. By this time several more of our friends had arrived, and they were all a little cautious as they approached me, mainly because I'd been one split pea soup incident away from *The Exorcist* only five minutes earlier.

After a few photos, the doctor announced it was time to push. At that moment some latent competitive urge rose up in me, and I determined that I was going to be the most efficient pusher Methodist Hospital had ever seen. Maybe they'd even put up a plaque in my honor: Hardest Pusher. Nurse Louise offered to bring a mirror around the end of the bed so I could see what was going on, but I declined. There are some things you can't unsee, and I felt like a baby coming out of my business end fell wholly in that category. Let's not go there.

After several pushes, between which I announced loudly how I'd really worked to keep my core muscles strong during pregnancy, Perry saw some things I desperately wish neither of us had to know about. But then I decided it probably helped the case I was going to make for why we should never experience marital intimacy again.

Finally I heard the doctor say, "I see her head," followed shortly by, "She's here!" And in that brief moment, life changed. There was a seismic shift where things went from being about me to being completely focused on the tiny, little creature who had just entered the room at 2:14 a.m. on August 3. I held my breath as the nurses carried her to a little incubator to check her out and take her vitals, and I finally breathed out again when the doctor announced, "She's a healthy little peanut."

And she was a little peanut. Only five pounds, eight ounces, but healthy and pink. They wrapped her up and handed her to Perry. He brought her to me, and I stared in wonder at this little pink gift, this tiny person fresh from heaven. It was as if I could still smell the angels on her, like I was looking straight into the face of God. A God who had just blessed us with so much more than we ever could have imagined.

How amazing that he brings life this way. Through pain and hurt and the ugly things inside us we try to keep hidden away. The things we don't talk about. In that moment, as I looked at my little girl lying in my arms, I realized this whole process was such a striking picture of how Christ works in us. He takes our disappointments, rejections, and hard times, and he makes something beautiful. He creates life and shows us what beauty looks like in places where we look and see nothing.

He blesses us beyond our imaginations, in spite of all the broken roads we've walked. In fact, maybe he blesses us so lavishly because of all the broken roads we've traveled. As if to remind us that he sees us—really sees us—not just for who we are at any given moment, but for what we could be one day.

That's how I felt when I looked at Caroline Tatum Shankle for the first time. Overwhelmed, humbled, grateful. It didn't matter that she didn't have any eyelashes yet, which caused her to look a little like a frog-baby, or that Perry, as he admitted later, was looking at her thinking, *Well, at least* we'll *love you and think you're cute.* I looked at her and saw perfection. And love. And mercy. And grace. I had never seen the hand of God more clearly in all my life.

✳

Our friends came back in the room, and we passed Caroline around to each one of them and took a million pictures. I called my parents on the phone because they were still trying to make their way to San Antonio from Houston, thanks to Nurse Louise's proclamation that I wasn't really in labor, and told them Caroline had arrived and couldn't wait to meet them.

And then Caroline was back in my arms, staring at me with those wide, brownish-blue eyes with no eyelashes and a look that seemed to say, *So you're my mom? I hope you're up for this, sucker.* She never made a sound but stared without blinking at everything going on around her as if taking an inventory of the world and trying to figure out if it met her standards. Like she might want her money back or something.

After a while the nurses announced it was time to take Caroline to the nursery to get cleaned up. They took her away, finished doing some stuff to me that I really didn't ask about, and told me they were going to take me to my private room. Praise you, Jesus, for the private room. At least that part of my birth plan was intact.

As they wheeled me down the hall, we passed the nursery, where my parents had arrived and were looking through the window as the nurses took care of Caroline. I heard my dad say angrily, "It seems like they don't need to be that rough with her. I hope they know what they're doing." I called out to them as I rolled by, and they all waved at me briefly before turning back to give their total and complete attention to the baby. All of a sudden I was just the vehicle that had provided them with a grandchild. Nice.

Once I arrived in my sweet nine-by-six private room that we paid extra for, an angel disguised as a nurse came in to check on me and said I should get some sleep before they brought the baby back in. Everyone came into the room to tell me good-bye and said they'd be back first thing in the morning. Then Perry and I tried to close our eyes and sleep.

We were both exhausted yet so hyped up on new-parent adrenaline that it was hard to wind down. I just wanted to see my baby girl again and make sure she was real. This whole thing was starting to seem like a dream. Of course, it helped that I was still totally numb from the epidural, as evidenced by the fact that I kept trying to move a pillow on the bed that turned out to be my own leg.

Around 6:30 a.m. they brought Caroline in to me. They said she was struggling to stay warm since she had so little body fat. (A problem she didn't inherit from her mother.) So I dressed her in one of the six gowns I'd brought to the hospital, marveling at her tiny toes and chicken legs and praying I wouldn't break her. The nurse showed me how to wrap her up like a little burrito, and then I held her while I formally introduced myself. "Hi. I'm your mama," I said. "Welcome to the world, little monkey bean."

My parents and my sister, who had been dying to get their hands on the baby, were finally able to hold Caroline for the first time. I knew they'd always been proud of me, but I felt like I'd just given them the keys to a magical kingdom filled with rainbows and unicorns. Or in my dad's case, a kingdom where no one has to pay income tax and there are no bad drivers who neglect to turn right at red lights. They looked at her with so much love. It felt like life had just come full circle right there in that tiny hospital room.

All of a sudden I realized I was starving. Perry ran down to the hospital food court and brought me a new McDonald's invention called the McGriddle. It was essentially eggs and sausage between two pancakes that had been infused with artificial maple syrup flavoring, and it was the most delicious thing I'd ever tasted in my life. I felt like I could conquer the world as long as I had McGriddles and my family by my side. And also my sweet recovery nurse, who had introduced me to the wonders of ice packs that fit neatly inside mesh grandma underwear that the hospital supplied in abundance for only ninety-eight dollars a pair, according to our final bill. I believe I was on what some may call a labor-and-delivery high.

The next two days were a blur of friends and family coming by the hospital to visit and Perry watching a NASCAR race while he held his new daughter because "train up a child in her redneck ways, and when she is old she will not depart from them." We passed Caroline around and I turned her into my own personal baby doll, changing her clothes every chance I got, because a girl needs to appreciate a good wardrobe as much as she needs to appreciate Dale Earnhardt Jr. winning Talladega.

On our last night in the hospital things were quiet. All the visitors had left, and I told Perry he should go home and get some sleep in a real bed. The nurse brought Caroline to me for one last late-night feeding. I took in every single inch of her while she nursed, still in a bit of disbelief that she was really mine and that they were really going to let me walk out of the hospital with her the next day.

After she was passed out in a milk stupor, I unwrapped her so I could take in those little fingers and toes. I took off her hat so I could see her thick black hair. And I wept. I wept because she was so beautiful. I wept because she felt like redemption for so many mistakes I'd made. I wept because how do you thank God for such an indescribable gift?

Lord, let me be worthy of this.

Lord, don't let me screw this up.

Perry arrived at the hospital bright and early the next morning. We did our best version of waiting patiently for all the necessary discharge forms to get filled out and listened to a long lecture about car seat safety. Clearly they didn't know they were talking to the chief of the Safety Police. Perry had already put those plastic childproof plugs in every outlet of our house even though I assured him it would be months before our little girl would do much more than look cute.

Eventually they brought our baby to us, and the pediatric nurse hugged us good-bye as she said, "Y'all are so lucky. She is one of the most laid-back babies I have ever seen." I nodded my head in agreement as I chalked up that trait to my already stellar parenting. Obviously Caroline's laid-back nature was a tribute to the forty-eight hours I'd spent performing my mothering skills with excellence. This was going to be so easy.

So with all the confidence of two fools who don't know any better, Perry and I loaded Caroline into the car. And, yes, I rode in the backseat with her, because what if something happened on the ten-minute car ride home? Two days in, and I was already one of those helicopter parents you read about.

As Perry chauffeured us home, I realized that life had already changed so much. We were a family of three now. Three. Which is significantly more than two.

Especially when one of you doesn't know how to microwave her own dinner.

CHAPTER 8

That Time I Didn't Sleep for Four Years

WHEN I WAS little I wasn't the best sleeper. I can't remember all the reasons why, but I'd like to go back and tell that little girl to *go to bed* and enjoy it while it lasts. I suppose I was afraid of the dark, I needed a drink of water, I had to go to the bathroom. I would push the limits of bedtime until my parents were forced to start following through on their threats. Which was usually my indicator that it was time to shut it down for the night.

But then I turned into a teenager and learned to appreciate the value of a good night's sleep. It became an art form as I looked for new and improved ways to make my bed even more comfortable, as evidenced by the fact I slept on top of my bed inside a fleece-lined Garfield sleeping bag for most of my high school years.

Then in college I discovered the beauty of scheduling all my classes for late in the day, thereby creating a twofold brand of awesome: sleeping late and having plenty of time to watch *Days of Our Lives* before I had to be bothered with the foolishness of geology lab. Because how was I supposed to get excited over a bunch of rock formations if I didn't know whether Bo and Hope escaped from the remote island where they were being held hostage by Stefano DiMera?

(On a totally similar subject, Gulley does the best impersonation ever of Tony DiMera. She can still crack me up to this day by walking into a room and saying, "Hello, Father," in a distinctly bad British accent.)

(This is the kind of thing we worked on during college along with planning the perfect outfit instead of actually studying and probably explains why I graduated on academic probation.)

My love for sleep took a hit after I married Perry. He is a believer in the theory that sleep is just something you do to have enough energy for the next day. That belief, combined with his insistence on keeping the same hours as Grandpa Walton, put a serious damper on my sleep schedule. I'd stay up late, per my night-owl tendencies, and then he'd wake me up at the crack of dawn, wanting to engage in real conversations with actual words and eat a meal that people apparently call breakfast. I played along for about the first six months because I didn't want to appear lazy. But then the newness wore off and I couldn't fake it anymore. We had to have an honest discussion about how I really never cared to see the sun rise or talk before 9:00 a.m. And those things you call eggs? No, thank you.

The low point came one day about four years into our marriage when we were having the exterior of the house painted. It was—don't judge me—probably about ten o'clock in the morning, and the painter needed an outlet to plug in a sander or something. I'm not totally sure because I don't paint houses for a living. Anyway, he noticed our bedroom window was cracked open, so he took the liberty of opening it a little bit wider to access an electrical outlet. However, he couldn't reach it because the bed was too close to the wall. So he began to move our bed while I was in it to get it out of the way. And I was so embarrassed about still being in bed at ten o'clock on a Wednesday morning that I just buried myself under the covers and hoped he wouldn't notice me lying there in my slothful state.

This incident didn't cause me to change my ways. It just made me double-check that our windows were shut before we went to bed at night. And I feel I should clarify that I was gainfully employed during this time, but I had the great fortune of working in pharmaceutical sales, so I justified my hours with the rationalization that I was doing the doctors a favor by not showing up at their offices before eleven o'clock. This gave them time to see their patients, and it gave me time to let the two deep sleep creases on my forehead go away.

(If any of my former managers are reading this, I apologize profusely. I was young and stupid, and you probably shouldn't have hired me in the first place. But I tricked you by appearing to be excited and motivated by success.)

(I was smart enough not to mention in interviews that a huge perk of the job for me was not having to be any certain place at any certain time. That's not the kind of thing that gets your foot in the door.)

Anyway, the point is I love sleep. I love sleep like some people love ham sandwiches. I can taste it. If I wake up after a particularly good night's sleep, I'll spend that entire day looking forward to the moment I can get back in bed and do it all over again. There were so many times during my pregnancy when I would remark, "It's just so hard to get comfortable at night. I'll be glad when she's born so I can get some sleep." And all the mothers in the room would look at me with blank expressions and nod their heads, but I know now they were silently thinking, *Get ready, sister, because that baby is coming, and sleep is about to be relegated to the category of "things that are in your past."*

✳

It was a Tuesday morning when we walked into our house with Caroline for the first time. Appropriately enough, Guy the electrician and Paul the plumber were still there, finishing up a few last construction details, like installing our real kitchen sink. So I recruited Guy to come into the front yard and take a picture of Perry, Caroline, and me in front of the giant stork holding pink balloons and announcing Caroline's arrival.

(I feel like I should clarify it wasn't a real stork. Although that would have been awesome.)

(But I think you have to go to the zoo or Vienna to find a real stork. The only thing I've ever had from Vienna is their little sausages.)

For the first few hours of our arrival home, the house was abuzz with plumbers plumbing and electricians electricing and ten lords a-leaping. Friends brought over food and flowers, neighbors stopped by to see the new baby, and my mother-in-law continued to organize the kitchen that we'd left in disarray three days earlier. Meanwhile, Caroline was content to be passed around from person to person in between sunbathing in her bassinet to help with her mild case of jaundice.

Then evening came, and everyone went home. The house felt eerily quiet. Perry and I decided to eat the roast Gulley and her mom had brought by earlier, so we heated up two plates, rolled Caroline in her bassinet right up to the table, and sat down to eat. Perry blessed our food and gave a prayer of thanks for our little family of three. And then, just as we began to eat, "You Are So Good to Me" began to play on the stereo.

We both sat quietly, listening to the music and eating our roast until the song got to the chorus:

You are beautiful my sweet, sweet song
You are beautiful my sweet, sweet song
You are beautiful my sweet, sweet song
I will sing again

We took a quick glance at each other and began to cry. Both of us. Not just me. Right there in our dining room, we were overwhelmed by love and grace. Overwhelmed by this sweet, sweet song who lay sleeping quietly next to us, all wrapped in pink and sucking on a pacifier that was bigger than her face. It was as if God had just walked over to the table and sat down. It was a holy moment. A holy moment with a mixture of a lot of awe and more than a little fear about what we were supposed to do next.

✳

Since Perry loves few things more than a good strategy, he came up with a plan of attack for the night shift. "Grandpa Walton" would go to bed early while I'd keep my usual night-owl hours and give Caroline her last late-night feeding around 1:00 a.m. The problem with having a baby who weighed only five and a half pounds was that the pediatrician insisted she needed to be fed every three hours without fail for the first six weeks of her life. Which translates to having to wake a sleeping baby. In the middle of the night.

Word to the wise: have a big baby. It's totally the way to go. I knew I should have eaten more donuts.

After her 1:00 a.m. feeding, I'd go to sleep and set the alarm for 4:00 a.m., at which time Perry would come in to give her a bottle while I used the dreaded breast pump and went back to sleep until 7:00 a.m. There really is nothing that will put the spark back in your marriage like having your husband see the sleep-deprived, hormonal version of you bent over a mechanical breast pump machine at four in the morning. Possibly while crying.

In theory this system worked fairly well, but we'd forgotten the whole unpredictable newborn-baby component. We assumed she'd just eat and go back to sleep. Instead, she felt nighttime was the time to party and get out all the gas she'd held in all day long. So my precious 1:00 a.m. to 4:00 a.m. sleep window translated to a forty-five-minute catnap after factoring in the time I spent changing her diaper and pumping her little legs like she was riding a bike to get rid of her gas and then changing her diaper again and then swaddling her and rocking her back to sleep. Not to mention all the times she'd fall asleep while eating, which may have caused me to actually utter, "If I can't sleep, then neither can you, sister." Honestly, just talking about the whole thing right now is causing me to have post-traumatic stress symptoms. Is it hot in here?

One night, at about the two-week mark, I was rocking Caroline at two thirty in the morning and I just began to cry because I was so homesick for the hospital. It was so lovely there, what with all the nurses and staff who would take my baby for a few hours so I could get actual REM sleep. I wanted to go back to that world of pampering and mesh underwear and pain medication doled out on a regular basis.

And maybe it was a combination of the sleep deprivation and the hormones, but I was so sensitive to every little thing. Gulley told me she survived late-night feedings with Jackson by watching movies on the DVD player, but I quickly discovered I couldn't handle the stimulation. The only thing I could bear to watch was *Little Women* (the Winona Ryder version—I think it's the best) and VH1's *I Love the Seventies*. There was a time I was certain Caroline's first words would be "What's goin' down, Mr. Kotter?"

Part of our nighttime strategy was that whoever was on baby duty would sleep in the guest bedroom with Caroline in her bassinet right beside the bed. This would allow the off-duty parent to get maximum sleep benefits in the comfortable, dark master bedroom. There were many nights I sat in that guest bed holding Caroline and concocting a plan to run away to the nearest Westin for just a few days. Why the Westin? Because I knew they had those heavenly beds. That's all I wanted in life. A heavenly bed in a quiet, baby-free hotel room. Surely Perry would understand if I just packed my bags and left for a few days?

But then Caroline would open her little mouth wide in a yawn or do that newborn stretch thing where her entire back arched backward and her arms lifted above her head, and I was brought back to the world where I was someone's mother. Yes, I wanted sleep, but I'd already started to dread the day she'd start kindergarten, because I knew it would be here before I knew it. And I couldn't even talk about what I was going to do when my maternity leave was over and I had to go back to work. So I'd rock Caroline to sleep while I prayed that kindergarten wouldn't arrive too quickly and that she'd have friends and that I'd get some sleep and that we'd win the lottery so I wouldn't have to go back to schlepping around drug samples to doctor's offices.

I couldn't imagine missing one moment of this little girl's life.

CHAPTER 9

War Buddies

THANKS TO MY almost sleepless nights, I walked around like a zombie for most of the days. The only thing that saved me was my sister, Amy, and her love for her new niece. Amy didn't have kids of her own yet, so it was a complete novelty to her to come over and rock Caroline for a few hours while I showered and put on the cleanest pair of pajamas I could find from the bottom of the laundry hamper. Makeup and jewelry became a distant memory. I was dressing for survival and selecting garments that could take me from awake to nap in sixty seconds.

I began to dread the evenings because I was so tired and all I wanted to do was crawl in bed and sleep for, oh, I don't know, maybe more than two hours in a row. But I knew it wasn't going to happen, and I'd start to fall into a deep depression right after dinnertime as I thought about all the sleep I wasn't going to get that night. It didn't help that Caroline had suddenly come alive on us and was ready to fight for her right to party.

I would hang over the edge of her bassinet, patting her back and making deals with God about all the humanitarian deeds I would do if only he would make her go to sleep. "You can do it, Lord. I know you can do it. You can move mountains." I developed the ability to sleep while holding my hand over the edge of her bassinet to keep her pacifier in place because if the pacifier went down, that ship was sunk. These were desperate times.

Then there was the night I emerged from Caroline's nursery to find Perry watching *Tears of the Sun*, the most violent, horrific movie ever made. It pushed me over the edge. I can't imagine why I didn't find a movie about the slaughter of Nigerian refugees uplifting in my time of sleep need, but it launched me into a tirade of tears. "I can't do this," I wailed. "I am just so tired. And I want to run away to the Westin on the Riverwalk."

I think Perry was a little stunned that I'd developed a fairly specific escape plan, and he agreed to take the entire night shift so I could get some real sleep. Or at least so I could sleep until I had to wake up and use the dreaded breast pump so nothing exploded. And as it turned out, that was exactly what I needed—just a few continuous hours of sleep that didn't involve keeping someone's pacifier in her mouth or listening to her let loose with an explosion in her diaper while I debated on a scale of one to ten how bad a mother had to be to let her baby continue to sleep in her own poop.

The next day I talked to my friend Jamie on the phone. Jamie has two boys who are exactly 364 days apart. (It's safe to say that wasn't planned.) She listened to me cry over my loss of sleep and the death of a lifestyle that now seemed so easy and carefree. And she spoke some words of wisdom that totally changed everything for me. "I know you can't believe it right now," she said, "but a day will come when you will put her in bed at eight o'clock at night and you won't hear a peep out of her for almost twelve hours."

That simple statement filled me with hope for the future. Of course, eight years later I'm still waiting on that day. But I believe it will come eventually.

Oh, I kid.

Kind of.

But somewhere around the twelve-week mark, it seemed to get easier. Or maybe I'd finally acclimated to sleeping in three- or four-hour stretches. And so I decided it was time to establish some sort of real schedule.

I'd heard all about the importance of "the schedule" through-out my pregnancy. Friends handed me all manner of books on the topic. All of which seemed to disagree on the best way to get your baby on a schedule but equally emphasized that failure to implement a schedule was likely to produce a child who would grow up to be covered in tattoos and living in a van down by the river.

Some people said I needed to let her cry it out, while others said that was a sure way to guarantee she'd resent me later in life and have long-standing trust issues. Some books said she was supposed to eat, sleep, and play—in that order, and that order only. But this threw me into a frenzy because, *Oh my gosh, she fell asleep while she was supposed to be playing, and what do I do now? The whole day is ruined.*

Ultimately I ended up taking bits and pieces of advice from various books and friends along with applying a dose of common sense and worked to figure out what was best for us. There were nights I'd attempt to let her cry it out, and I lasted only four minutes before I caved and ran into her room. And then there were other times when I'd actually go through with the whole cry-it-out thing, which were usually the times I'd have to leave the house and put Perry in charge because my heart couldn't take it.

In spite of my lack of experience, the schedule happened. Through a combination of trial and error and teething and dirty diapers and why-is-she-still-awake moments, we developed a routine. Caroline had inherited her father's Grandpa Walton tendencies and was usually in bed for the night by 6:00 p.m. By the time she was five months old, she'd normally wake up once during the night and then go back to sleep until six o'clock the next morning. And I became a person I didn't recognize. A person who was excited by the prospect of sleeping in until the luxurious hour of 6:00 a.m. A person who saw sunrises every morning and heard the early-morning cannon go off at the nearby army base.

But those early mornings are the fabric of some of my sweetest memories from Caroline's baby days. We'd curl up on the couch and watch *Sesame Street* together because that was before "the experts" determined that television before age two ruins your child. (Clearly those experts never had a small toddler and a husband who likes to eat dinner every night. Because otherwise they'd collect a stash of Baby Einstein DVDs so fast it would make your head spin.)

She would relax against me with her arms propped behind her head like she was a fifty-year-old man relaxing after a long day at the office, and we'd laugh at Elmo and I'd sing her songs and my heart would ache because I loved her so much. I look back at those days and think that's exactly what people mean when they tell you the days are long but the years are short.

Those were the days I would look at the clock and couldn't believe it was only eleven in the morning. Those were the days I'd count down the minutes until bedtime. But those were also the days that seemed to be gone in the blink of an eye.

Sometimes I regret that I didn't enjoy them more in the moment, but isn't that the way motherhood goes? Looking back, the sweetest things are often the hardest things. They teach you a level of sacrifice you didn't know you were capable of, and for me, having a child was the beginning of a glimpse into the kind of love Christ has for us. Sacrificial love. Love that doesn't keep score. Love that isn't dependent on what's in it for me. Love that is consuming and protective and unconditional. These are the early moments that bonded me forever to Caroline because we were like war buddies. There was a feeling of, *Hey you, we survived another day.*

Those are the days I walked around feeling like the end-of-the-movie version of the Grinch—my heart that was once small grew at least three sizes. And I wouldn't have missed one of them for all the sleep in the world.

Unless it was on really high-thread-count sheets.

CHAPTER 10

Back to Work,
Back to Reality

THE BEAUTY OF being employed in the pharmaceutical sales industry was that it came with a sweet six-month maternity leave. Granted, not all of it was paid leave, but I had the luxury of plenty of time to adjust to life with a new baby before having to figure out how to incorporate a full-time job into the equation. Honestly, I don't know how women do it when they have to go back to work after just six weeks, when their boobs are still leaking and they've had a total of four hours of sleep since the baby was born.

Before I had Caroline, I had a master motherhood plan in that cute, naive way all women have of believing they can map out their futures without factoring in hormones and blinding love. We'd found a nice, older woman who was willing to come to our house five days a week to look after Caroline and maybe even cook the occasional homemade enchilada dinner while Perry and I worked. Her name was Stella, and I just knew she was going to be the best thing to ever happen to our family. She even came by to meet Caroline while I was on maternity leave and told me that the magical cure for a baby with hiccups was to put a piece of red string on her forehead. How could I not feel comfortable about someone with that level of baby expertise taking care of my child?

But as the days of my maternity leave wound down, I began to question whether I could have another woman in my house with my baby. It had seemed like such a good idea in theory, but the reality was I wanted to be home with Caroline instead of delivering Chinese food to an angry doctor's office staff. But that wasn't really an option at the moment. We needed the insurance and the free car my job provided, and there wasn't any other choice.

However, I began to realize that with Perry owning his own landscaping business and my being in sales, we had fairly flexible work schedules. So I tearfully presented him with the suggestion that we let Stella know she wasn't needed and just make the whole parenting thing work between the two of us. He agreed.

I called Stella to let her know we weren't going to need her or her homemade enchiladas after all and explained that it wasn't her; it was me and all my conflicting emotions about attempting to balance a motherhood I adored and a career that I didn't really care about but had to endure because of the regular paycheck.

It was early February when I began my stint as a working mother with a full-time job. It was hard enough just being away from Caroline during the day, but then I was informed

I'd have to fly to Chicago for four days of meetings. I felt like my heart was going to break. The morning I left, my mother-in-law came to watch Caroline while Perry drove me to the airport, and I stood in my kitchen and cried my eyes out. I regretted our decision to renovate our house and spend all that money. Why couldn't we just live in a shack so I could stay home and be with my baby? Why did I think we needed to have an electrical system that didn't short out every time we ran the microwave?

But then my mother-in-law, a woman not inclined to show much sympathy for melodrama and self-pity, looked at me as I tried to stuff my laptop into my bag between sobs and said, "You need to get over it."

Wow. Well, that was certainly harsh. I wanted to yell back, "Why don't *you* get over it?" but that didn't really seem to have any relevance in this particular situation. So I just let Perry steer me out the back door and into the waiting car before I said something I would most likely regret.

But as mad as the comment made me, I slowly, slowly began to realize she might have a point. This was my new reality. I'd always known I'd have to go back to work at some point, and I could either embrace it or resent it. And so I embraced it. Mostly. I spent those four days in Chicago missing Caroline terribly but at least halfway admitting to myself that I'd forgotten what a luxury it was to get in bed at ten o'clock at night and sleep nonstop until seven o'clock the next morning. I hadn't been that rested in six months.

And so began two years of shuffling meetings and coordinating schedules and not performing my job nearly as well as

I should have. My heart was always at home, and I no longer cared at all about doctors and prescription drugs.

(As opposed to the days when I cared so much that I was still in bed at 10:00 a.m. when the painters arrived.)

To say those were a long, hard two years is like saying I might be interested in a chocolate donut when I'm suffering from PMS. It was a constant juggling act. Perry and I would sit together with our calendars every Sunday night and play schedule roulette as we bargained and haggled over whose meetings were more important and whether or not the Smiths' new driveway really needed to be poured on Tuesday because I was supposed to deliver breakfast to Dr. Garcia and his entire staff that morning.

It didn't help that Caroline had decided at some point around the one-year mark that sleeping through the night was overrated. Why sleep when you can stand in your crib and see how far you can throw your pacifier? I would run that child like she was training for a marathon during the day in an attempt to get her to sleep all night, but she would still call me into her room at 3 a.m., and how was I supposed to resist a little monkey in footy pajamas saying, "Rock you, Mama," which was her way of asking to sit in the rocking chair with me for just a little while.

Another of her favorite middle-of-the-night activities was a game I liked to call "You Find It, Mama," where she would call me in with a cry of distress to ask me to find her pink bunny or Squeak E. Mouse or any other stuffed animal that was guaranteed to be located at the very bottom of the toy box.

No, please don't worry that your mother hasn't experienced

a REM cycle in six months—let's make sure we find Blue Shaggy Dog at four in the morning.

There was a point during this time that I went to the dentist hoping I had a cavity just so I could have an hour or so to sleep in the chair while it was filled.

✳

Eventually I began to realize we couldn't go on this way. Perry's landscape business was growing, and I couldn't keep doing my job halfway and completely sleep deprived. That's when I began to explore the wonder known as preschool. Caroline was almost two, and I felt like the fall would be a great time to put her in school for a couple of days each week.

I visited a few local church schools, including the one Perry had attended as a little boy—the one everybody claimed was the best—which is where I ultimately enrolled her. The headmistress had been around since God was a child, and I was convinced that her serious approach to a child's education and overall development would be the best thing for Caroline. When the headmistress described the school's distinctions to me, she informed me how important it was for each child to bring a nutritious, well-balanced lunch to school each day and commented that one little boy even brought brussels sprouts. I went home and announced all my findings to Perry, including the bit about the kid who brought brussels sprouts. He said, "Oh, yeah, that was Jason Miller, back when I was there. He's always been a total freak."

Of course, I underestimated a few things in my school decision, such as Caroline's love for peanut butter and jelly with a side of Cheetos and my fundamental belief that a serious approach is a boring approach that can suck the life out of a person. Because it's all well and fine that your school is accredited by the blah-blah board of blah-blah, but preschool is really more about learning basic social skills than the Keynesian theory of economics. Let's not take people who still poop in their pants too seriously.

Sometime in late August I packed Caroline's new Nemo lunch box with what I hoped passed as a fairly nutritious lunch, though there was nary a brussels sprout to be found, and walked her to her new little classroom. At the time she seemed so big to me, but now I look back at pictures and wonder why on earth I was dropping an infant off at preschool. She was still just my chubby-cheeked baby, with her bouncy ponytail and her Keds with Velcro straps.

I counted down the minutes until it was time to pick her up at 2:45, anxious to see how her first day had gone. I was astounded when I walked into her classroom to discover that she was asleep on her nap mat. The teacher explained she had taken forever to fall asleep and had spent much of that time distracting the other kids before she finally passed out from exhaustion.

I scooped her up, her hair matted to the side of her sweaty little face, and carried her out to the car. As I asked her about her day, she told me she'd had fun but she didn't like nap time. Which should have come as no surprise, considering she wasn't a fan of naps, or sleeping in general, at home in her own bed, so why did I think she was going to relax on an inch-thick mat with her shoes still on in a classroom full of kids?

I spent the rest of the evening worrying about the nap-time

dynamic at preschool, and my fears were confirmed the next morning when I dropped Caroline off at school. Her teacher met me at the door with the announcement that I needed to pick Caroline up prior to nap time because having her there was too disruptive for the other kids.

Seriously, lady? You gave us one shot at nap time, and we're out? I found it hard to believe Caroline was the only child who struggled with the nap. But I agreed to pick her up before nap time, and that's what I did for the next three weeks until Caroline decided she didn't want to leave school early anymore. I explained that meant she'd have to lie down and sleep at school, that she couldn't keep the other kids awake. She agreed, and from that point on she made it through nap time with only a few issues here and there. It was hard for me to be a fan of her teacher after the whole napping debacle, but Caroline loved her and even named the baby doll Santa brought that Christmas Mrs. Laurie. And how could I argue with that?

I mean, doesn't it say in the Bible that no greater love hath a toddler than naming a baby that wets its diaper after her preschool teacher?

CHAPTER 11

Potty Training: Bringing People to Their Knees Since Forever

PRESCHOOL BECAME A normal part of our lives. Caroline loved getting to see all her friends several times a week to make crafts and eat paste and fight over tricycles, and I was able to better balance having a career and being a mother. We adjusted. I accepted that being a working mother was what God had for me, and I was okay with it. But in my heart my prayer remained the same: I wanted to be home. I wanted to have time to bake cookies and have lazy mornings watching Bert and Ernie with a snuggly girl in pajamas who wasn't going to be little forever.

Which brings me to an important milestone in any motherhood career.

Potty training.

I know.

Somewhere, someone just groaned as they read those words.

That's because potty training a child is the equivalent of teaching a cat to tap-dance, and there are CEOs of large corporations who have never felt that level of accomplishment. When Steve Jobs, founder of Apple, passed away in 2011, there was much talk about how he changed the world. And, yes, it's incredibly clever that I can ask a device smaller than my hand where the closest Starbucks is or what the weather will be like the next day, but there is no app that will convince your child to enjoy the benefits of indoor plumbing as opposed to sitting around in her own excrement.

For the first year of a baby's life the diapers aren't so bad. I mean, yes, there is the occasional blowout that requires a gas mask and a team of people to get it cleaned up, but that's part of the parenting deal. But it all gets a little more complex when your precious baby can walk up to you and announce, "Mama, I poo-poo in my diaper." Because if you can claim it, then you should have the wherewithal to do something about it. Not to mention the implications of a dirty diaper that belongs to someone on a steady diet of chicken fingers, hot dogs, and macaroni and cheese.

(Not that Caroline ever ate a steady diet of any of those things. We were purely organic at our house.)

(If you consider organic to mean anything that comes in the shape of a dinosaur.)

(In my defense, it's hard to think about cooking a healthy, well-balanced meal for a child who has been known to live on a single cheese cube for days at a time.)

Truth be told, I hadn't given much thought to potty training. It was a vague destination in my mind, someplace we might venture at some point when I felt brave or had a prescription for Xanax. Perhaps we might toy around with the idea the summer before Caroline turned three. Maybe we'd get one of those plastic starter potties and let her get used to the idea of sitting on it; maybe we'd get her some magazines to read, since that seems to be what works for her father.

But then the very serious preschool where kids eat brussels sprouts threw me for a loop.

One day in May I opened up Caroline's little Nemo backpack to find a note announcing that all children must be completely potty trained by the age of three or they would not be promoted to the three-year-old class. There would be no exceptions.

You can rest in the knowledge the whole thing sent me into a tailspin.

All of a sudden I had only three months to get us all aboard the potty train. And I had a child who showed absolutely no interest in taking this step toward independence and proper hygiene. But now her academic future depended on it. She was going to get held back if she couldn't get rid of the diapers. My baby girl was going to fail the two-year-old class. Her future as valedictorian of preschool was at stake even though she'd recently learned all her shapes and how to count to ten. Unless you count the times she skipped over six and seven.

I headed to Target that very day to acquire a plastic potty and a copy of every storybook I could find about people who use potties. Look! Ernie uses the potty! Princesses use potties! Everyone uses the potty! Potties are the new black.

That night I made a big deal of introducing Caroline to the

new potty I'd placed in her bathroom right next to the adult version. I explained it was her very own special potty and that she was the only one who got to use it. Whenever she felt like she needed to go tee-tee, she could let me know and we'd race in there and use her very special potty.

She looked me dead in the eye and said, "No thank you, Mama." And then she picked up her very special potty, carried it into the living room, and proceeded to use it as her personal lounge chair for the next two weeks. I kept hoping she would eventually grow to appreciate its function, not just the obvious comfort of the plastic backrest, but I hoped in vain. I became convinced Caroline was determined to be the first child who would go off to college wearing a Huggies Pull-Up.

✳

A few weeks later I was talking to my friend Deidre at work and perhaps singing a chorus of "Swing Low, Sweet Chariot" as I lamented our potty-training troubles. Deidre had two daughters in elementary school who appeared to be totally potty trained, plus I knew I could count on her to be honest. After all, she'd told me a few days earlier that my new aviator-style sunglasses looked terrible with my face shape. I didn't feel like she'd be afraid to be up front about my lack of potty-training expertise.

Deidre said the problem was we needed to go cold turkey. No more diapers, no more Pull-Ups, no more couch that doesn't smell like urine. She said the trick was to put Caroline in big-girl underwear and then set a timer for every thirty minutes and take her to the bathroom. Because, sure, it wasn't like I had anything to do other than clean stains off my rugs and cry every thirty minutes.

But I figured it couldn't hurt to try it since my method of praying and begging God for mercy didn't appear to be working out. I drove back to Target to acquire some pretty My Little Pony underwear, because attractive, child-appealing underwear was an important part of the equation, according to Deidre. The next morning I showed Caroline her new underwear and told her that the pretty pony with the pink mane would die if it got any tee-tee on it.

I didn't really say that. But, oh, I thought about it.

I made a huge deal of the responsibility that comes with beautiful underwear and told her we'd work together to make sure she remembered to use the potty. And we made it through the first day with only one minor accident. Then we made it through the second day with no accidents. And then, on the third day, she actually began to tell me when she needed to go to the bathroom without waiting for the timer. And then I threw away my new aviator-style sunglasses because clearly Deidre was a genius and knew what she was talking about.

Praise Jesus! My baby was going to pass the two-year-old class. She was going to make it after all, just like Mary Tyler Moore. Someday we'd be able to pack her bags for college and not have to explain to her new roommate why she had a case of Huggies in the back of her dorm room closet.

But my celebration was short-lived when I realized there was still an issue. While Caroline had mastered the art of tee-teeing on the potty, she had yet to poop on the potty. In fact, she outright refused to do so. It took me a while to figure it out because I am very slow, but it began to dawn on me that she had trained herself to wait to poop until I put on her nighttime Pull-Up right before she went to bed. I'd get her out of the bath and put on her lavender-scented lotion, her Pull-Up, and her sweet little footy pajamas with the pink monkeys all over them. Then we'd cuddle up in the rocking chair in her room and read bedtime stories. Shortly thereafter she would excuse herself to "go tell Daddy night-night" and come back to me five minutes later smelling like a sewage plant.

After about three nights of this, I followed her into the living room as she went to tell Perry good night and discovered that she made a quick pit stop behind the armoire that houses our TV to do her business. All red-faced and squatting behind the armoire. Like she needed her privacy to poop in the Pull-Up her mother was going to have to change three minutes later.

I desperately tried to outsmart her by changing up our night-time routine. I'd wait to put on her nighttime Pull-Up until the last possible moment, after I'd given her more than several opportunities to go do her business on the toilet. But, oh no, nothing beat the comfort of the Pull-Up. You know how you hear about those primitive tribes in the jungle somewhere who won't let you take their picture because they're afraid it might steal their soul? That's how Caroline was about her poop. As if letting that part of her go down the pipes was the equivalent of saying good-bye to her very soul.

Meanwhile the clock was ticking on our back-to-school date and whether I'd be able to truthfully tell the serious preschool that Caroline was completely potty trained. I reasoned that she was completely potty trained between the hours of 8:45 a.m.

and 2:00 p.m., and that's really all they needed to know. What happened in the privacy of our home and my child's Huggies was our personal business.

So I signed her up for the three-year-old class and initialed on the dotted line that she was, in fact, completely potty trained. Thankfully there was no official exam or anything. But I did receive a note a few days later informing me Caroline's new teacher would be making a home visit prior to the beginning of the school year. Naturally I requested that her visit be sometime in the morning hours.

So Mrs. Green came to visit. My first indication that things weren't going to go well was when Caroline decided to hide under the dining room table. Even at three years old, Caroline never passed up an opportunity for social interaction. It wasn't like her to not want to entertain our guest with all manner of musical instruments and conversation.

Mrs. Green appeared to be very warm and personable, so I decided to take this opportunity to question her about the dynamics of bathroom politics at the school. "How does that work? Do you help them at all? Like if they need help pulling up their pants or buttoning a button?"

"No," she replied with a smile. "We really encourage completely independent toilet abilities. All children should be able to wipe their own bottoms and button their own pants." Good night, am I raising a rocket scientist? What three-year-old can wipe her own bottom and button her own pants every time? I know some grown-ups who are still working on those skills.

Mrs. Green went on to explain that there wasn't a bathroom in each individual classroom but rather one bathroom located in the courtyard area of the school. She said the teachers usually sent a group of kids to the bathroom at the same time, and that way they could help each other if needed.

Well, sure. That sounds like a brilliant plan. A bunch of three-year-olds whose parents have most likely embellished their potty-training abilities for fear that they won't make the Ivy League all going to the restroom together. Why not just send in a group of monkeys and call it a day? The whole premise seemed fraught with potential disaster.

While I was privately pondering the serious preschool's bathroom etiquette, Caroline continued to hide under the dining room table. She had no interest in Mrs. Green or the stuffed animal she'd brought in an attempt to break the ice. After a while we gave up, and I walked Mrs. Green to the door and thanked her for her time. And shortly thereafter discovered that Caroline had taken that opportunity to poop in her pants.

That's when I got on the phone and began to call around to other preschools to beg, borrow, or steal any potential openings for a three-year-old girl who could kind of/possibly/not every time go to the bathroom by herself but who was in general really cute and terribly charming.

Which is how we ended up at a new preschool that didn't take itself too seriously. A preschool that realized kids enjoy peanut butter and jelly a lot more than brussels sprouts and occasionally need a little help wiping their bottoms or buttoning their pants and that none of these things are really indicators of who's going to qualify for Mensa membership in the future.

CHAPTER 12

We Don't Throw Sand

THE OTHER DAY I was on the phone with a customer service representative from AT&T, which means I am playing fast and loose with the term *customer service* right now, but that's not the point. Anyway, I heard myself say, "Yes, ma'am, thank you for scheduling an appointment for me to get my Internet fixed in two weeks with a six-hour window of uncertainty. I really appreciate it." When everything in me wanted to scream, "Are you kidding me? Two weeks? And you can't narrow down a time frame to less than six hours? You are dead to me. Just like my Internet."

But I didn't say that, because my parents taught me appropriate social skills and I've mostly learned to suppress what I'd really like to say in favor of something that's more polite. It's one of those things you take for granted. Until you have a child of your own, you forget that all of us come into this world with a completely selfish nature that makes us inclined to scream, "No! It's mine!" at any given opportunity.

All that to say, Perry and I had really given no thought to how we would attempt to teach Caroline appropriate social skills. And it's really one of those things we should have thought about, considering our daughter comes from two parents who have been known to speak first and think later.

In fifth grade I once got detention because I didn't think my PE coach had kept score correctly during a game of kickball and I made the mistake of loudly declaring, "Three plus two equals five, and if he doesn't know that, then maybe he should go back to fifth grade." Shortly thereafter, I found myself sitting in the office of our principal, Mrs. Archer. Which is a whole different story because she had these long, talon-like fingernails that still make me feel a little bit afraid when I think of them.

Mrs. Archer called my parents to tell them about my smart mouth, and I ended up grounded for the next week. But I learned an important lesson. Watch what you say to a man who probably had dreams of coaching college football and instead ended up wearing polyester coaching shorts that are too tight and refereeing a bunch of ten-year-olds as they play kickball.

I wish I had some great wisdom to impart about how to teach your child appropriate social skills, but the jury is still out on this. At least twenty-eight times a day I tell Caroline, "Tell her thank you," or "Make sure you say, 'Yes, ma'am,'" or "You need to apologize for leaving that popsicle to melt on top of Daddy's toolbox." But there are still plenty of times I hear her tell a friend, "NO! I don't want to play that game!" or "You're not invited to my birthday party!"

And we all know there is no greater insult in the world of elementary school than the threat of rescinding a birthday party invitation. Even if the party isn't for eight more months.

*

When Caroline was about a year old, we began to work on teaching her to say "please" and "thank you." And she got pretty good at it. We patted ourselves on the back and felt like we were doing a pretty good job. Check out our adorable little fifteen-month-old with her impeccable manners. She says "please" every time she wants another piece of banana. We believed we might be raising the next Emily Post.

And then came our first summer at the neighborhood pool, when the dodgy politics of the baby pool came into play. If you think I'm kidding, it's because you've never spent much time around a baby pool. All the mothers walk in loaded down with crab floats and princess tea sets and pushing their precious toddlers in strollers. Toddlers who just happen to be dressed like senior citizens on a beach in Miami, complete with enormous sun hats.

It's all fun times until you actually take your baby out of the stroller and she enters the treacherous waters of the baby pool, where the kids think everyone else has the best toys . . . until they see someone else playing with their crab float and unceremoniously yank it out from under the poor, unsuspecting child who was relaxing on it (probably while peeing in the pool, because let's not kid ourselves about that). All the while they're yelling, "No! It's mine! Mine! MINE!"

In the meantime the mothers are all shocked and horrified by this behavior because why would our children behave this way? Never mind that every single one of us might get into fisticuffs with someone who dared to go into our closet and wear our new boots since they're "mine! Mine! MINE!" We are perplexed because it's just a crab float, not the pair of new Frye boots we've been coveting for the last three years.

But we wade into the baby pool to help our children navigate this new social terrain because that's our job, and we smile at our fellow mothers as we do our best to be polite even while we're thinking that maybe Harrison's mother should drag in her own crab float next time if Harrison so obviously feels his life isn't complete without it. Why should our child be punished because Harrison's mother wanted to stroll into the pool unencumbered by a large, inflatable member of the crustacean family?

Gulley texted me from the baseball fields the other day because she recognized a mother in the stands whom she'd had a slight altercation with at the baby pool years ago. Now their boys are on the same baseball team, which is just another example that God has a sense of humor. Gulley said, "Do you think she remembers I told her maybe she could go buy her own alligator float for $5.99 at Target?"

Because that's the whole problem. While we're trying to teach our children appropriate social skills, we sometimes lose our own. All our protective mama-bear instincts come out, and we're quick to see the speck in another child's eye while perhaps ignoring the plank coming out of our own.

✳

Caroline had a big issue with throwing sand when she was a toddler. If there was a sandbox within a two-mile radius, it was a guarantee she would find it, dig in it for a few minutes, and then throw sand directly at the nearest unsuspecting victim.

Around this time Gulley and her family moved to a house about a mile away from us, which was a dream come true for two college roommates who had always dreamed we'd be able to live nearby and raise our kids together. And we relished this new proximity to each other with almost daily playdates. Our thought was that my daughter, Caroline, and Gulley's boys, Jackson and Will, were going to grow up to be best friends, whether they wanted to be or not.

The only problem was that every time we went to play at Gulley's house, the kids always made their way out to the huge sandbox in her backyard. Inevitably Jackson or Will would run up crying to report, "Caroline threw sand at me! She threw sand!"

I would march out to the sandbox and ask, "Caroline, did you throw sand at the boys?" She would look me right in the eye and announce, "Yes, I throw sand." I'd yank her out of the sandbox while declaring, "We don't throw sand. Do you understand? We don't throw sand at our friends. It could get in their eyes and hurt them. They could end up blind." (I believe situations that could potentially cause blindness are an important tool in the motherhood arsenal. Threatening blindness or a trip to the emergency room usually produces results.)

The sand problems with Caroline became an almost weekly occurrence until I finally placed a temporary ban on the sandbox until the time arrived that she could resist her temptation to throw sand.

About a month after the previous sandbox incident, I was out of town on a business trip. Gulley had picked up Caroline from preschool and was keeping her at their house until Perry could get her after work. He arrived a little while later and sat out in the back with Gulley while the kids played in the sandbox. Sure enough, our little sand thrower couldn't help herself, and the boys came running up to Gulley, announcing, "Caroline threw sand! She threw sand at me!"

Perry looked right at Gulley and said, "Oh, I'm sure she didn't mean it. I don't think she knows she's not supposed to throw sand."

Hi. Are you new here?

In Perry's defense, he hadn't been a part of the weekly sand drama and didn't really know the severity of the situation, but I think it shows our inclination as parents to always want to see the best in our children. We like to believe they are better versions of us, but the truth is, they *are* us. They are full of our selfishness and impulsiveness and pettiness. They want things to go their way just like we do, and they scream and yell and throw things when it doesn't work out. The only difference between them and us is what my grandma would refer to as "home training."

God gives us these raw, little people, and we have to form them and mold them and teach them how to operate in society. And if we get a glimpse of all the ugliness that lies right beneath our own polished surface? Well, then, there's a humbling lesson too. It's those moments when I realize I have to extend grace to Caroline as she figures these things out by trial and error in the same way God lavishes me with mercy, even as I make the same mistakes over and over again.

CHAPTER 13

Letting It All Hang Out

WHEN PERRY AND I moved into our house in the spring of 1998, we discovered that our neighbor Tillie had lived in her house since the 1950s. Actually her name was Adeline, but according to the story she told us, back in the 1940s, when her husband was in the war, she drove herself around town in spite of the fact that she didn't know how to drive. Her driving skills led the priests at her parish to nickname her Rootin' Tootin' Tillie. The "rootin' tootin'" part went away, but Tillie stuck.

We first met Tillie when she hobbled over to bring a tin of assorted chocolate candies to welcome us to the neighborhood. She knew a good thing when she saw it, and it wasn't long before she was calling Perry to come change lightbulbs, hang her US flag, and do other assorted jobs. She never actually called him Perry; she called him Terry, which made it all the funnier when she'd call us to request that Terry fix her clothesline or undertake whatever the chore of the day happened to be.

Tillie's husband died when they were seventy, and she'd been a widow for twenty-six years. Although she never had children of her own, she had a niece and a nephew who came over to take care of her. They weren't necessarily a lot of help, seeing as how they were eighty. Every Sunday they would pull up to take her to church in their Caddy with the Kleenex box in the back window, and it was almost painful to watch them all get in the car. You could never quite tell who was helping whom, and after her eighty-year-old nephew began wearing a neck brace, he'd just pull out from the curb without ever looking to see if a car was coming. Perry and I would just hold our breath watching the whole scene unfold.

Pretty soon after we moved in, Tillie began calling me to take her to run errands. We'd head out to the Hallmark store so she could stock up on cards for all her great-nieces and great-nephews. I can't tell y'all how many hours I spent standing in Hallmark while Tillie opened every single card and LOUDLY read them to me. This always led to my prayers for serenity as Tillie read, "To a dear niece, you are loved more than you know."

Then she'd say, "Oh, I don't know if that sounds right. I'm not sure she's loved more than she knows. She knows she's loved. Her parents have spoiled her until she's totally rotten."

And I'd stand there, trying to be patient, thinking that Tillie was never going to find a card that read, "To a dear niece who knows how much she's loved because her parents spoil her rotten and bought her a BMW for her birthday and it's total foolishness and it symbolizes everything that's wrong with kids today." Because Hallmark really fails to reach that particular demographic.

On the way home from Hallmark, we'd usually stop at the HEB, which is our local grocery store. Tillie had never gotten over the fact that the HEB used to be a Handy Andy and would always tell me, "Honey, you could even buy your underwear at Handy Andy, and I am always in need of new underwear." Tillie had reached the point in life when you can just air all your thoughts and no one really thinks twice about it. And if they do, you don't care.

I'll never forget our first trip to HEB, when I helped her get a basket and she assured me I should just go ahead with my shopping and we could meet at the register. I zipped through the store, got everything I needed, and came back to find Tillie about one aisle from where I had left her. From then on, I always walked through the store with her. One of my greatest memories from these trips is when she cornered the store manager and went on and on about how you can buy cheese in cubes or slices or any other such foolishness, but "Why in the world can't you just buy a block of rat cheese?"

He had this blank look and questioned, "Rat cheese?"

She replied, "Yes, you know, like you put in a rat trap to catch a rat."

"Ma'am, are you needing to catch a rat?" he asked.

She looked at him like she couldn't believe she was having this conversation and said, "Of course not. I'm needing to eat some cheese. A block of rat cheese."

Perry and I started taking her out to eat about once a week. One night we were at a neighborhood Mexican restaurant where

Tillie had eaten for years. When our waitress came to take our order, Tillie told her, "Honey, I hardly recognized you because you've gotten so fat."

I wanted to crawl under the table, but Tillie told me, "Honey, she needs to know. She has gotten fat, and I'm just being honest." I've never been more certain that a waitress spit in our enchiladas before serving them.

The priests from Tillie's parish came to visit her on Sundays, and she'd always talk about how they liked to drink her vodka. In fact, she claimed that drinking vodka was part of what had kept her alive for so long. Sometimes she'd start to lose her balance while we were out, and she'd say, "Honey, I can't remember if I'm drunk or just old."

A few years later Tillie had to have her gallbladder taken out. After she got home from the hospital, I went over to visit and she insisted on showing me her incision because, "Honey, you just won't believe it, they just take it out through your belly button. Have you ever heard of such? Through your belly button."

And as I tried to protest that I didn't really need to see it, she lifted up her nightgown to show me her belly button, and let's just say that gravity isn't kind to you when you're ninety-nine years old, so along with her belly button, I saw other parts of her anatomy hanging down there right next to it. Oh yes, ma'am, Tillie and I knew each other well.

A few years after we moved into our house, my former hairdresser and his life partner moved into the house behind ours with their two adopted girls from Cambodia, a seventy-year-old Hispanic housekeeper, and a Filipino nanny. Their house was clearly visible from Tillie's house, and one day as we were headed to Bun 'n' Barrel to pick up a barbecue sandwich, Tillie pointed to their house and said, "Honey, that is an ODD assortment of people that live in that house. What do you think is going on over there? I can't figure out who goes with who."

God bless her.

Anyway, for years I wondered why God had brought Tillie into our lives, and once I had a child who became a toddler, I quickly realized at least part of the reason why. He was preparing me for what life is like when you are with someone who has no desire or inclination to filter their every thought.

Because as much as they need to learn not to throw sand, they also need to learn you might not need to say everything that pops into your head.

One day when Caroline was about two, we went to the park. I watched her go down the slides and play on the various playscapes, and then she said, "Come on, Mama! Let's go swing!"

I put her on one swing, and I sat down on the swing next to her, even though I noticed it had a little dried bird poop on it. No big deal. I'm a gamer like that. I laugh in the face of bird poop.

(Not really. I don't even know what that means.)

After a few minutes, she said, "Let's switch swings, Mama!" So, we got off our respective swings, and she walked over to mine, looked down, and yelled, "OH, MAMA! DID YOU POOP IN YOUR SWING?" As if I were her incontinent mother who makes a habit of pooping on playground equipment.

Then there was the day I was sitting in the kitchen with a Bible study workbook and my Bible, pen in hand. The very picture of studious. The portrait of a godly woman.

Caroline could sense that I was having a moment to myself, so she came over to see what was going on.

"What are you doing, Mama?"

"I'm doing my Bible study."

"Oh, I'm going to do my Bible study too!"

She climbed up on the bar stool next to mine, grabbed a pen, and started scribbling on a notepad. I watched her for a few moments and thought, *This is what it's all about. I'm showing her my love for Jesus. I'm creating an example of living a life dedicated to God, and how precious that she wants to model that behavior.* And secretly, I even wished the other person who lives in this house (that would be Perry) would notice this moment of mother/daughter/God closeness and take a picture of the sweetness.

I went back to reading my study when Caroline said, "Mama?"

"Yes, my precious angel baby darlin'?"

"I just drew this picture. It's a picture of what my poop looks like."

See? No filter.

* * *

A while back Caroline had the croup. She couldn't get to sleep, and I could hear her hacking away in her bedroom in spite of the cough medicine I'd given her earlier that evening. She finally came out of her room in tears because she felt so bad and couldn't go to sleep.

And so began a marathon of every home remedy I knew and some I didn't know but learned thanks to Twitter, which is a better resource than WebMD because it's filled with mothers and no one is telling you that every little symptom is a sign of cancer.

I sat with Caroline on the front porch so she could breathe in the cold night air, rubbed Vicks VapoRub on her feet, sat with her in the rocking chair, gave her a teaspoonful of honey, and sang her lullabies in spite of my bad voice.

Finally I ended up turning on the hot water in the bathroom with the hope that the steam would help. I sat on the toilet lid with her snuggled on my lap while the thick steam enveloped us. She seemed so little and delicate, and my heart just hurt because I could tell she was miserable. I rubbed her feverish back and encouraged her to breathe in the steamy air to help loosen up all the "fungus" (as she called it) in her lungs. After a few minutes she pulled away from me, put both her hands on either side of my face, and looked at me closely.

"Mama?"

"What is it, baby?"

I thought maybe she was going to tell me she still didn't feel good. Or maybe say she loved me.

"Mama?"

"What, love?"

"I'm not saying this to be mean, but it's time for you to do something about your mustache. I just thought you might want to know."

Well. I did not see that coming.

But you know what? I did want to know. I needed to know. Because I'd obviously been walking around for weeks with a little too much facial hair. Perry wasn't going to tell me because he hates sleeping on the couch. Gulley might have said something, but she knows me well enough to recognize that could lead us down a whole rabbit trail filled with my insecurities. We'd start with my need to get my upper lip waxed and end up somewhere in the neighborhood of "Am I fat? Be honest. Do you think I need to lose ten pounds? Be honest." Even though we all know that no best friend is going to say, "Yes, I've been meaning to tell you it's time to drop some weight, sister. You are bordering on wide load."

(If I'm wrong and you have a friend who told you that, then I'm going to gently suggest that you find some new friends.)

But kids will tell you, because they haven't learned to filter everything out. And maybe that's okay sometimes. Sure, you can't go through life throwing sand and drawing pictures of poop, but what if we were all a little more transparent? What if instead of pretending something didn't hurt our feelings, we'd say, "You know what? That hurt my feelings." And then we could work it out instead of letting it simmer under the surface until the bitterness chokes us.

My sister, Amy, told me she was worried about my niece, Sarah, starting kindergarten last year because she just wasn't sure about Sarah's social skills. Amy was afraid Sarah wouldn't be ready to interact with the other kids in the right way. Amy said, "Sometimes at the park I'll see her walk up to other kids she doesn't know and say something weird like 'My jacket has four pockets. How many pockets do you have?'" I assured her that all kids are just a little bit bizarre and half those kindergartners will eat a whole tub of paste before the school year ends, so I wouldn't really be concerned about what constitutes appropriate. The year Caroline was in kindergarten I volunteered in the school cafeteria, and there were kids who drank the leftover juice from their pinto beans with a straw. Bean juice. With a straw. In light of that, I think asking someone about the number of pockets in their coat is completely acceptable.

So, yes, I think we need to teach our kids to say please and thank you and you're welcome. And if you live south of the Mason-Dixon Line, then I think they should say, "Yes, ma'am," and "No, sir." Maybe they should do it up North too, but I don't live up North, so I don't really feel qualified to comment on that. In the words of Suzanne Sugarbaker from *Designing Women*, "Having bad manners is worse than having no money." That's some wisdom right there. But maybe we can take a cue from the toddlers in our lives and not filter out all the real parts.

They aren't going to get it right every time, but neither are we. Our job as mothers is to do the best we can to teach our children that life is better and friendships are richer when we treat others with kindness, when we remember to share, and when we use nice words. To remember that every person we come in contact with may have a few cracks in their hearts even if we can't see them and that love is always the best response.

But it also might be better if everyone kept their belly buttons and at least some of their thoughts to themselves.

CHAPTER 14

I Can No Longer Bring Home the Bacon

WHEN CAROLINE WAS three, I received a call from my manager informing me the Human Resources department had some questions related to my work performance. They needed both of us to fly to Dallas so they could question me and/or fire me in person.

The issues in question were completely false and due to computer error. I knew this and my manager knew this, but my fear was that this lady in HR, who didn't know me from Adam, wouldn't grasp this and there wouldn't necessarily be a way for me to prove anything.

The best part was that they scheduled this career-deciding meeting a full week and a half from the initial phone call, which really allowed an abundance of time for me to do what I do best: completely freak out.

I got off that phone call with my manager, and in 2.8 seconds I had us living on the streets with no health insurance. I am, by the way, an insurer's dream come true because I'm just paranoid enough to sign up for any policy within a five-hundred-mile radius.

I am obviously a risk taker by nature.

So I hung up the phone and walked out to tell Perry about the call. Given the fact that all the blood had drained from my face and I was hyperventilating, he intuitively knew something very bad had happened, such as losing my job or overplucking my eyebrows again.

As the news of our imminent homelessness came pouring out of my mouth, he sat and listened to me. When I was finally drained of words, he looked at me and said, "It will be okay. God's in control."

Umm, yeah. I knew that.

And the thing is, I did know that. But in that moment and throughout the following week and a half, there were times when I completely forgot. I let fear grip me instead of letting God's peace envelop me.

In short, I was the Bode Miller of Christian faith. Remember Bode Miller? That skier in the 2006 Winter Olympics who was supposed to win all the medals? He was highly trained, he had tons of experience, he was the media favorite. But when it came time for the biggest event of his career, he choked. He didn't win one medal.

That was me. I had experience. I'd walked with Christ for years. He'd carried me through the lonely days of being a new college graduate in a town where I knew no one, through bad job situations, through the deaths of people I loved, and through a heartbreaking miscarriage. I'd watched him bless me with a great husband, a beautiful daughter, wonderful friends, and a happy home. I knew him. I'd tested him, and he had always proved faithful. Always.

Yet I was so quick to prove faithless. One unexpected turn, and I was down for the count. In the Olympics of Christianity, I wasn't even going to get a bronze medal.

After the meeting it became apparent to everyone that all the allegations were false, and I came home from Dallas knowing my job was secure for the time being. But something had shifted. This whole turn of events served as a catalyst for me to think bigger than myself, to quit looking at what I could tangibly see, and to take the leap of seeing my life and my potential through God's eyes. I realized how much I'd been walking in fear and trusting myself and my ability to provide instead of trusting God.

A few weeks later I was watching an episode of *Friday Night Lights* (which, incidentally, is the best show that has ever been on television, and I still mourn for it to this day). At the end of the episode, Tami Taylor finds out she's pregnant. The nurse asks her, "Honey, do you want this baby?" and she replies, "I prayed for this baby twelve years ago and then eleven years ago and then ten years ago and finally realized that God must have other plans." The nurse looks her right in the eye and says, "Well, honey, it looks like God changed his mind."

And I began to cry.

I cried because I knew how it felt to pray and get an answer. I knew how it felt to hope that God would change his mind.

And the irony is, while I was watching that show, I had no idea what God was about to do.

My manager called me the next day and told me it appeared my job might be in jeopardy after all. The weird thing was that, as she talked, I felt perfectly calm.

In fact, I remained so calm I wondered if I was having some kind of breakdown that was preventing me from properly computing information.

Perry got home and we talked about it. He asked me if I thought this was God's way of pushing me to take a step of faith and resign from my job. He put into words exactly what I was feeling. I knew it was time to walk away.

It all came together in the right way, at the right time.

Perry and I sat and talked about everything, and we couldn't believe the peace we felt about this decision. After three years of questioning why, I suddenly saw the hand of God's timing and provision. We were at a point where Perry's business was becoming more consistent, and I was making tens of dollars from some freelance writing opportunities. Plus, we'd had a few years to accumulate more in our savings account like real grown-ups.

Don't get me wrong—it wasn't like everything was just perfect. There were huge obstacles, like the seasonal nature of Perry's landscape business and the loss of my company car, our sweet insurance, and a nice, dependable check that was direct-deposited into our checking account every two weeks. We were jumping into the deep end and trusting God to an extent we never had before. And it was scary.

Yet I was so grateful God had changed his mind, and over

the next several months Psalm 16:5-8 took on a whole new meaning for me:

> LORD, you alone are my portion and my cup;
>   you make my lot secure.
> The boundary lines have fallen for me in pleasant places;
>   surely I have a delightful inheritance.
>
> I will praise the LORD, who counsels me;
>   even at night my heart instructs me.
> I keep my eyes always on the LORD.
>   With him at my right hand, I will not be shaken.

I resigned from my job a few days later with trembling and fear but also with excitement to see what God had in store for us. It was the beginning of my new career as a stay-at-home mom.

After a few weeks of being home, I decided to compare how I spent my days as a pharmaceutical rep with a day spent as a stay-at-home mom.

Drug rep: *6:30 a.m.* Wake up to the sound of a belligerent three-year-old yelling, "Mama, come get me! It's *morning!*"

SAHM: *6:30 a.m.* Wake up to the sound of a belligerent three-year-old yelling, "Mama, come get me! It's *morning!*"

Drug rep: *7:00 a.m.* Stumble into the kitchen and try to come up with something she'll actually eat for breakfast while she begs for candy. Listen to her throw a fit after I say that a York Peppermint Pattie isn't really a breakfast food.

SAHM: *7:00 a.m.* Stumble into the kitchen and offer several breakfast options, all of which are turned down because they aren't York Peppermint Patties.

Drug rep: *8:30 a.m.* Load myself up like a pack mule headed for a ten-day camping trip in the Grand Canyon. With one shoulder, support Caroline's school bag, my purse, my work bag, and my laptop bag. In the other hand, carry her lunch box and my car keys. Follow her out to the car while she stops to examine every crack in the sidewalk, look at every bug, and give the dogs a hug good-bye. Finally get to the car right before my arm falls off from the sheer weight of items I'm toting.

SAHM: *8:30 a.m.* Stay in our pajamas for a little while longer because we can. Watch *Charlie and Lola* and continue to push my breakfast agenda. She is so over breakfast. Breakfast is for the weak.

Drug rep: *9:00 a.m.–12:00 p.m.* Spend morning trying to convince doctors who already know everything why they should use my drug instead of my competitor's drug. They pretend to listen while I know they are completely ignoring everything I'm saying.

SAHM: *9:00 a.m.–12:00 p.m.* Spend morning trying to convince three-year-old who already knows everything why she shouldn't color on the walls, run with sharp objects, or spill her cereal all over the kitchen floor. She pretends to listen while I know she's ignoring everything I'm saying.

Drug rep: *12:00–1:00 p.m.* Have lunch delivered to doctor's office so I can have the pleasure of treating office staff and physicians to a free lunch while they complain that they've already had Jason's Deli this week and ask why I didn't bring more Diet Dr Pepper.

SAHM: *12:00–1:00 p.m.* Make peanut-butter-and-jelly sandwich; deliver it to three-year-old so I can have the pleasure of making her a delicious lunch while she complains that she's already had peanut butter and jelly this week and asks why I didn't give her pink lemonade.

Drug rep: *1:00–2:00 p.m.* Take a nap.

(I'm joking. It's a joke.)

(Everyone knows drug reps don't take naps from 1:00 to 2:00 because they finish their day by 3:00 and go home and take a nap then.)

SAHM: *1:00–2:00 p.m.* Take nap and try to get Caroline to do the same.

(Or at the very least, not to wake me up.)

Drug rep: *2:00–4:30 p.m.* Go see more doctors and bring them free samples of drugs while most of them act put out that they must acknowledge my presence. Some of them enjoy asking me difficult questions that I don't know how to answer, such as the particle size of the LDL and apoB lipoproteins.

Umm, yeah, I majored in speech communications.

SAHM: *2:00–4:30 p.m.* Go to the grocery store and buy food for Caroline while she acts put out that she must acknowledge my presence. She enjoys asking me difficult questions that I don't know how to answer, such as how do watermelons turn green on the outside.

Umm, yeah, I majored in speech communications.

Drug rep: *5:00–bedtime.* The day is over, with the exception of an occasional evening when I get to go out on the company's dime to some of the nicest restaurants in town and eat good food and drink fine wine while listening to some of the most boring presentations known to man.

SAHM: *5:00–bedtime.* I still have miles to go before I sleep. Dinnertime, bath time, and bedtime routines. There are chicken nuggets to be eaten, hair to be washed, and stories to be read. I wouldn't trade it for the best meal in town at the nicest restaurant, even without the boring presentation.

Although the wine would be nice.

Drug rep: *Middle of the night.* Wake up completely stressed out about how I'm going to grow market share when the only way I'll be able to convince some of these doctors to write my drug is if they undergo a complete lobotomy.

SAHM: *Middle of the night.* Wake up completely stressed out about how I'm going to fill all the hours in the next day with meaningful activities that don't include watching *Backyardigans* over and over again.

As you can see, in some ways my days weren't that different. The commonality between being a drug rep and being a mama is that before I actually started being either one, I read a few books. I studied, I learned all I could, I memorized material that could help me in any situation and allow me to answer any question.

But the thing is, only the reality of doing something every day prepares you for what it's really like. No book can tell you how to make a doctor prescribe your drug, and no book can tell you how to get a toddler to eat her breakfast. It's all a game of skill and chance. Some days I got it right, and some days I didn't. Some days I think I've got it all figured out, and some days I'm sure I must be the most incompetent person to ever attempt this job.

From my perspective, I'm just thankful that if I'm going to spend my days with someone who ignores half of what I say and acts like she knows better than I do, it's my daughter. Because for all those moments she is so over me, there are those moments we spend digging for worms, lying on the floor coloring pictures, and playing Go Fish.

Those are moments I wouldn't trade for anything.

Plus, most of my doctors were terrible at Go Fish.

CHAPTER 15

Putting the Crazy on Display

HERE IN SAN ANTONIO we have an annual two-week celebration called Fiesta. It allegedly has something to do with Texas's independence from Mexico, but I think it's really just an excuse for everyone to take off work and for the socialites to wear crowns and pretend they're real royalty. There are always parades and various foods served on a stick and coronations and multiple stabbings by angry drunks. Good times.

Caroline's preschool liked to celebrate Fiesta by having the kids create their very own shoe-box floats. The teachers sent home a note regarding all the Fiesta activities they had planned for the kids. I know it seems that a visit from real, live royalty in the form of King Antonio would be more than enough, but it's not. A visit from King Antonio would have required little to no parent suffering, which was just not acceptable.

The note went into great detail about how each year the kids make these floats and how it is such an enjoyable experience for the teachers and kids that many parents requested that they be able to make this a family project to be done at home.

Who are these parents?

No one would fess up, for fear of being ostracized from the preschool community.

So while there was technically still the option of having your child make the float at school with the help of the teacher, the implication was that you could either spend hours with glue-and-glitter-coated fingertips or hang your head in shame after essentially admitting you were an uninvolved parent whose child tucked herself into bed each night while you and your husband sipped martinis in the living room.

Now don't get me wrong. I don't like to publicize it, but I secretly love a good craft project. The problem is not with the craft in and of itself; the problem is I know it will unleash my OCD tendencies. I know I won't rest until I have glittered and tissue-papered and decorated within an inch of my life because we all know that three-year-olds have the attention span of a flea in a dog pound, and if I wanted Caroline to pull a float that consisted of more than a shoe box with a Hello Kitty sticker on it, it would be up to me.

I immediately sold Caroline on the idea of a Wizard of Oz–themed float because McDonald's was giving out Wizard of Oz Happy Meal toys at the time. I envisioned a miniature Oz-themed paradise, complete with darling Madame Alexander Happy Meal figurines standing under a glittered rainbow.

The problem was every time we went to McDonald's, we got

Dorothy or the Munchkin. No Wicked Witch, no Tin Man, no Scarecrow. I hated to be high maintenance at McDonald's (which is fairly ironic, considering it doesn't really bother me to be high maintenance anywhere else) and ask for a specific Happy Meal toy. I just kept playing the drive-thru like I was at a craps table in Vegas, hoping my luck would change.

As the due date for the shoe-box float drew near, I realized I was in trouble. First of all, I had four Dorothys and two Munchkins. Then when I dropped Caroline off at school a few days before the floats were required to be in, I saw a few of the other finished floats on display. These floats belonged to the kids whose parents had relinquished float-making duties to the teachers because they were much smarter and more aware of their issues than I was. When I saw how good those floats looked and noticed that one even included Spiderman scaling a skyscraper, I began to hyperventilate just a little. Something inside me kicked in, and I knew it was time to bring my float-making A game.

OCD is real, people. It is a sickness.

After I left Caroline at school, I immediately drove to Michaels to secure the materials I would need to make the best float ever. I bought colored tissue paper, foam board, decorative flowers, and enough glitter to outfit a chorus line of Vegas showgirls. The missing link was the other characters required to complete my Wizard of Oz masterpiece.

Then, as if in answer to prayer, Gulley called and said she was taking Will to ride the train and pick up a Happy Meal at McDonald's. I hate to use the word *beg* because it sounds so desperate, but yes, I begged her to request the girl toy in the

Happy Meal and, if she wouldn't mind, to please specify that she'd like a Wicked Witch or a Tin Man.

So while I hated to appear high maintenance at McDonald's, I had no problem asking my best friend to not only ask for a specific toy but to cheat her son out of a Happy Meal toy. But he was only two, and I justified it by telling myself he wouldn't know the difference and, if he did, I'd pay for the therapy.

Gulley called me about twenty minutes later with news. And it wasn't good. The McDonald's closest to us had run out of all Wizard of Oz characters and instead was offering My Little Ponies.

There was no way I was giving up on the Wizard of Oz float just because some moron at McDonald's didn't order enough Happy Meal toys. Don't try to pawn off your My Little Ponies on me, high school boy. Everyone knows those are left over from the last giveaway.

I am embarrassed to admit that I called a few other McDonald's locations looking for the Wizard of Oz figures and finally secured a Scarecrow. I actually had the girl hold it for me (so much for not being high maintenance) and went and picked it up.

I realize I am in need of professional help.

That night I wrapped the shoe-box float with green paper, made a yellow brick road out of glitter, and placed Dorothy and the Scarecrow on top. (Yes, Caroline was asleep in bed for all of this. What? Like she was going to help with her own float?) I quickly realized I needed a Tin Man and a Lion. I searched through the playroom and found a lion left over from some other Happy Meal. Granted, this lion didn't look like he needed much courage because he was striking a jujitsu pose, but he'd do. Then, in a flash of brilliance, I decided to turn one of the Munchkins into a Tin Man using some foil. I got out the Reynolds Wrap and went to town. I posed the Lion and the Munchkin Tin Man next to Dorothy and Scarecrow and went to bed.

The next morning Perry walked in the kitchen, looked at the float, and asked, "What does a foil alien baby have to do with *The Wizard of Oz?*"

He is a gem.

Finally, after too many hours of cutting, glittering, and gluing, the float was finished. As I carried it into Caroline's classroom that Thursday, I started to worry that maybe I had done too much. Maybe my OCD had gotten completely out of control. Maybe my float would be so good that other parents would be embarrassed about their own paltry efforts.

But as soon as I arrived and placed the shoe box in the lineup with the other creations, I realized that while the Wizard of Oz float was a valiant effort, it was by no means the best float in the parade. These parents took their floats seriously. Very seriously. As opposed to me, who was so completely normal about the whole thing.

Which made me think we might all be like the Scarecrow and in search of a brain. Or at least something else to do with all the time we apparently had on our hands.

The whole experience was a turning point for me. I can laugh about it now, but at the time I was overwrought. It was a lesson in trusting my own instincts concerning my daughter. Just because you feel pressure from other people about the way something should be done, it doesn't mean it's the best thing. Sometimes you simply have to go with your heart and believe you know your child better than anyone else does.

And that there comes a time when you should just slap a Hello Kitty sticker on a shoe box from Payless and call it good.

CHAPTER 16

Lifestyles of the Sick & Feverish

YEARS AGO WHEN I started working as a pharmaceutical sales rep, people warned me that I was about to be sicker than I'd ever been in my life. Sitting in all those doctors' waiting rooms was the equivalent of hanging out in a giant petri dish with nothing but bad carpeting and an aquarium to entertain you during a ninety-minute wait, they warned. And while I did have my share of coughs and colds during those years, those bugs pale in comparison to the illnesses I have lived through in my tenure as a mother.

There's a lot of talk in the news about homegrown terrorists, specifically the threat of bioterrorism. Well, I hate to be a fearmonger, but if those terrorists really want to take down an entire country, they can find everything they need in the classrooms at the local preschools.

Now, I will admit I'm a bit of a germophobe. I cringe when someone drinks out of my glass, and although I try to act all *Whatever, I am so casual and cool with this* when someone uses my fork to try a bite of my food, everything inside me is screaming, *Alert! Alert! Bacteria! Bacteria!*

Perry and I have some good friends we used to go fishing with on a regular basis. Actually, they fished. I really just held a fishing pole while working on my tan and thinking about new ways to fix my hair. Anyway, Kevin is a total germ freak. As in, he makes me look normal and well adjusted. He doesn't even like it when his wife drinks out of the same beverage after him. The thing is, when you're out fishing in a boat all day, everyone usually just throws their Gatorade back in the cooler and does their best to grab the one that belongs to them each time they need a drink.

But Kevin always marked his Gatorade. Because he didn't want to risk sharing germs even with the woman he has vowed to love forever. And so we all respected his Gatorade ways and made sure we avoided his bottle.

One afternoon we had been out in the boat all day. It was hot and still, and I think we'd caught maybe two fish among the four of us. I didn't really care because my tan was looking marvelous, but everyone else was getting a little cranky.

About that time Susan pulled an apple out of the cooler and began to eat it. When she finished, she took that slobbery, wet apple core and chucked it right at him as she yelled, "Apple core! Baltimore!" Perry and I watched in horror as that nasty apple core hit him right in the side of the face.

It was one of those moments in my life that I'll always relive in slow motion. If there was ever a time I'd considered jumping into the dark, scary ocean and swimming for shore, this was it. Perry and I wanted to disappear.

Kevin looked up, wiped the slobber from his face, and yelled, "What on earth did you do that for? What were you thinking?" And, realizing she'd just made a huge tactical error, Susan mumbled, "Don't you remember that game 'Apple core! Baltimore!' where you throw an apple core at someone?" Unfortunately, she was the only one who'd ever heard of that particular game. Which is understandable because you have to admit it's a horrible premise for a fun-filled activity.

Anyway, that happened at a point in my life when I wasn't nearly as paranoid about germs, but now that I've reached my current level of neurosis, I can fully appreciate the horror of a spit-covered apple core hitting you in the face. Sometimes there just isn't enough sanitizer.

The thing is, when you first bring your baby home from the hospital, you're hypervigilant about everything. Everyone who walks through your door has to be hosed down with anti-bacterial gel. You invest in bleach and boil pacifiers. You see everyone as one big mass of bacteria waiting to infect your precious baby. My friend Jamie boiled the plastic toys lining her son's ExerSaucer until the little puppies and dinosaurs were nothing but misshapen blobs. Basically, you turn into a total freak. You're like Howard Hughes but in sweatpants and a nursing bra.

Eventually I realized that pacifiers can be boiled only so many times and that if Caroline could survive being kissed on the lips by the dog, then she could probably withstand a little dirt on the baby spoon she'd just dropped on the floor for the fifteenth time in four minutes. Not to mention she had a real penchant for gumming the handle of the grocery store shopping cart every time I turned my back. It was like she was determined to contract the plague in spite of all my best efforts.

But she was born with a strong immune system and never really got sick as a little baby. Yes, there were a few stuffy noses that required those blue sucker bulbs of torture, but no fevers or anything some little saline nose drops couldn't cure.

Until she started preschool.

Or as I call it, the all-inclusive germ resort. Where else do people believe it's totally acceptable to take the toy out of your friend's mouth and put it in yours? Or that playground sand is the perfect snack item when you get a little peckish before lunch?

It was a memorable Thanksgiving when Caroline came down with her first real illness. I was a little annoyed because she refused to eat any of her Thanksgiving lunch, and who refuses to eat Thanksgiving lunch? It's the Super Bowl of food. I mean, I would have understood if she just didn't want turkey, because I have my own various issues with poultry, but no broccoli-rice casserole? No dressing and gravy? No chocolate icebox pudding for dessert? How can this child have come from my body?

But shortly after lunch was over, I stretched out on the leather couch at Mimi and Bops's house to take a postlunch catnap. And that's when Caroline toddled over to me, climbed right up and lay on my overstuffed stomach, put her face right by mine, and said, "Mama? My mouth feels funny."

All I managed to say was, "What do you mean, your . . . ?" before her little body made a heaving motion and I found myself covered in throw-up. It was all over both of us. In our hair, on our clothes, all over the couch. And I thought, *Well, it will clearly be easier to just set ourselves on fire than attempt to clean this up.*

One thing was sure: I'd never before found Thanksgiving lunch to be so completely unappealing.

We did our best to clean up the mess—at least the best you can do without a fire hose full of bleach—and took our sick little girl home. Where she proceeded to throw up every thirty minutes for the next six hours. The worst part was that a toddler doesn't really understand the concept of running to the toilet every time she feels the need to yak. Not to mention she was completely traumatized by the entire experience (yes, join your mother as she deals with post-traumatic stress disorder—maybe we can get a two-for-one deal in a therapy program), and she just wanted me to hold her every time she started to throw up.

About the sixth time I had to do a complete wardrobe change after holding her in the vicinity of the bathroom while she threw up, Perry announced we needed a more efficient system or I was going to run out of ratty old shirts.

(Little did he know I could never run out of ratty old shirts because I am a shirt hoarder. I have shirts that precede my college days, and that was, lo, many years ago.)

(Also, only Perry would try to devise a more streamlined throw-up system. Like the real problem was we just weren't organized enough with our gastrointestinal issues.)

Caroline couldn't grasp running to the toilet or just lying on the bathroom floor enjoying the feel of the cold tile on her face, which has always been my preferred method of dealing with stomach illness and/or too much fun in the aforementioned college years.

So the next time she looked up at me from the couch I'd covered in beach towels and announced, "I feel my fro-ups coming, Mama," I picked her up, opened the front door, and held her out over the railing of our front porch. I'm sure the neighbors were delighted with this display. Nothing like a little post-Thanksgiving exhibition of complete foulness by a two-year-old wearing nothing but a diaper, and her mother, who's wearing a 1991 Diamond Darling Christmas Formal shirt that says, "Deck the Halls with Bats and Balls!" The sweet, naive college girl who wore a velvet dress with hot-pink sleeves bigger than her head to that Christmas formal never could have imagined the atrocities that shirt would see fourteen years later.

And so Perry spent the next morning hosing down the bushes in our front yard while I succumbed to the dreaded stomach virus myself and lay on the bathroom floor wishing I could just die and mentally composing my last will and testament.

(I was going to leave my CHI flat iron to Gulley.)

In the true form of a child, Caroline had made a complete recovery. She danced around me as she asked over and over again, in a singsong voice, "What's happenin', Mama? What's happenin' in your mouth, Mama? You so sick, Mama?"

Yes. Mama is sick. Largely because she spent the last twelve hours covered in throw-up that wasn't her own.

Mama is going to die now. But you rest in the comfort of knowing it was very important that you chewed on the handles of that tricycle at preschool and contracted heaven-knows-what and brought it home to roost.

I don't know if this is in any of those books about parenting, but if I had to give you a definition of what motherhood really looks like, I might just say it's a woman who catches her child's throw-up. With her bare hands.

CHAPTER 17

Nitpicking

SINCE THE INFAMOUS Thanksgiving flu incident, we've experienced a variety of illnesses courtesy of our little rhesus monkey. Most of them have been your typical stomach virus/cold/bronchitis/strep-type thing. And of course Perry and I would both end up with some version of all of these, which led to our very own Symptom Showcase Showdown, in which contestants compete to see who feels the worst.

Then came the morning Caroline climbed into my bed and announced she had a sore in her mouth. And I noticed she also had little blisters on her hands. This earned us a diagnosis of hand, foot, and mouth disease by the pediatrician.

The great irony is that many years before, in my prechild days, I'd attended a business meeting and had to share a room with a girl I'd never met before. (Yes, that is a situation that is thirty-one kinds of awkward anyway.) She was a sales rep in Minnesota or somewhere like that and became really sick the second day of the meeting. When I went back to our hotel room that night, I found her lying on the bed, sweating from fever, and she showed me little blisters on her hands. I think I said something calm and soothing like, "Oh my word, I think you're going to die."

But she told me she knew it was hand, foot, and mouth disease because her son had it before she left on the trip. At which point I found my manager in the lobby of the hotel, grabbed him by his collar, and whispered desperately, "Listen to me. You have got to get me my own room. My roommate has some weird disease called hand, foot, and mouth, and I don't know what that is, but I'm pretty sure you get it from rabid, dirty sheep. I beg you, please get me my own room."

It was exhibits A, B, and C of God's sense of humor that now my very own child had come down with this horrible illness that makes people believe you've been spending time on unsanitary farms. The reality is, it's just a normal virus-type thing and fairly common.

On the upside, Caroline slept for about three days straight because she was so tired. However, on the downside, she walked around for the next six months telling anyone who would listen about all the sores she had in her mouth. And then I'd feel the need to overexplain that she no longer had sores in her mouth but she'd had hand, foot, and mouth disease several months ago. Which caused the cashier at the grocery store to look at me like she wished I'd just go back to the place with the dirty sheep from whence I'd come.

But the plague that almost took us down and caused me to search the Internet for inpatient treatment programs was the great lice outbreak of 2011. I'd spent the last weekend of July at the beach with a group of my best girlfriends. It was an early celebration for my upcoming fortieth birthday, and we'd had the best time.

(Well, except for the part where we almost got arrested by the policeman working the line at the ferry because he gave us a ticket we felt was uncalled for, and my friend Julie wasn't afraid to let him know it.)

(In case you're wondering, the use of sarcasm rarely, if ever, endears you to police officers.)

I walked through the back door relaxed and refreshed and generally in love with my life, thanks to how special my wonderful friends had made me feel all weekend long. Turning forty was going to be awesome. Caroline walked into the bathroom to watch me unpack my bag, and I noticed as she bent down that she had a rash on the back of her neck. It suddenly dawned on me that I also had a rash on the back of my neck.

So I asked her, "Does that rash on your neck itch?" She replied, "Yes, it itches really bad." I did what I do in all life situations that involve a potential medical mystery: I consulted Google, just knowing there was at least a 95 percent chance that an itchy rash on the back of your neck is a symptom of cancer. Because Google loves nothing more than a cancer diagnosis. It's the reason I've lost countless nights of sleep worrying about whether or not my yellow tongue was a sign of liver cancer.

(It wasn't. It was a sign I needed to step away from the Christmas sugar cookies and eat a vegetable every now and then.)

(So I didn't have liver cancer, but I was on the verge of scurvy.)

As it turned out, an itchy rash on the back of the neck is a symptom of lice. I immediately began to pick through Caroline's hair and, sure enough, nits. *Nits.* My head is itching right now just thinking about it.

We both had lice. And I spent the next several days soaking our heads in mayonnaise, olive oil, and lice treatment options from the drugstore. At one point I seriously contemplated just pulling up to a gas station, paying at the pump, and dousing our heads with unleaded premium.

Everything on the Internet said you needed to bag stuffed animals, spray everything you own or have ever looked at with Lysol, and wash all bedding in hot water. I just wanted to sell the house fully furnished and move. Honestly, it seemed easier. Turning forty was going to be a living nightmare.

But I persevered and combed out nits in Caroline's hair while Perry combed out nits in my hair. We spent our evenings just like a family of monkeys at the zoo. It was a real treat. Make that thing #4,753 on the list of things you never imagine, as you walk down the aisle in the beautiful white dress looking like a fairy princess, your husband will have to do for you.

It was shortly after I'd declared our household lice free that Caroline threw me under the bus at church one Sunday. I don't mean she literally threw me under the bus. I want to clarify because our church does offer a shuttle bus from the parking lot, and technically a person *could* get thrown under the bus at church.

I mean she sold me out.

She had become friends with a little girl in her Sunday school class, and the girls were playing after church while the adults stood around and visited. This little girl's father, whom I'd never met, walked up and introduced himself to me. About that time, Caroline joined in the conversation, and he asked if she was an only child. She told him she was, and he mentioned that his daughter was an only child too, and sometimes she got bored at home.

While I listened in horror, Caroline said, "Yeah, me too. I get so bored. I ask my mom to play with me, but all she does is sit on the couch. She's real lazy."

I'm sorry? I'm real lazy? Last I checked I was ridding your hair of the plague and pestilence you picked up from who-knows-where and spending my evenings looking for microscopic eggs.

I desperately wanted to defend myself to this man I didn't even know, but I knew anything I said would just make me sound more guilty. So I stood there frozen, torn between wanting to redeem my mothering, throwing my child under the literal shuttle bus, and running to the car and bursting into tears because I suddenly felt like a total failure.

Instead I opted to say in an overly cheerful voice, "Okay! Well, you have a great Sunday!" I proceeded to grab Perry, telling him it was time to go, and I couldn't even look at Caroline. As soon as we got in the car, I turned to her tearfully and said in a shaky voice, "Is that what you think of me? That I'm lazy and don't do anything for you?"

She looked at me like a deer caught in the headlights as I went on. "How many moms go on every field trip? How many moms eat lunch at school with their kids almost every week? How many moms help with spelling tests by making the letters with their whole body like they're doing the 'YMCA'?"

Meanwhile, Perry wasn't sure what had just happened. He was staring at me like I'd lost my mind as I sobbed and went into general hysteria. But I think he got the gist because he pulled over the car and told Caroline, "I don't think it was very nice to say your mom is lazy. I don't think you realize or appreciate how much she does for you."

Then Caroline burst into tears and said, "I'm sorry, Mama. I'm sorry. I don't even really know what *lazy* means. I just meant that sometimes you get tired from taking care of me and have to take a break."

Well, that is the truth, sister. That is the truth.

I spent the rest of the day feeling a little shell shocked. All I've ever wanted to be was the best mother I could be, and I felt like my daughter had just announced to the world that she didn't feel like I was doing a great job. Everyone I told this story to assured me I was a wonderful mother, but there are some wounds that just take a while to knit back into wholeness. To be honest, my pride was hurt more than anything.

I think I'd been living under the illusion that I could give Caroline a perfect childhood. But perfect doesn't exist in our world. I can give her love, I can give her laughter, I can instill values and morals in her, I can teach her about Jesus and how he loves her more than she knows, and I can hopefully give her more good memories than bad.

And I can pick the nits out of her hair, one little larva at a time.

But I can't give her perfection, because I'm fresh out.

That's where the grace of God enters, and I exit quietly through the back door, allowing him to fill in the gaps.

CHAPTER 18

Ready for the World

I REMEMBER MY first day of kindergarten. Actually, I don't know that I remember the actual event so much, but I've seen pictures of it that help me know things I can't recall from real memories. I wore a red dress and navy blue Keds, and I rode the school bus. Then at the end of the day I forgot to get off the school bus, and the driver didn't realize it until a few blocks later. I do kind of remember that part. The panic of knowing I wasn't supposed to still be on the school bus but not being sure what I was supposed to do about it.

Little did I know it then, but that moment was just the beginning of so many times I'd feel that way—insecure, panicked, and afraid that I'd really screwed everything up. Welcome to the real world. It's a kick in the pants.

And maybe that's why I'd been dreading the moment

Caroline would start kindergarten ever since the day she was born. I didn't want to send my baby out of her safe little cocoon and into the big, bad world of kindergarten. I wanted to keep her safe and make her feel secure. And most of all, I wanted to be in control of everything she would ever hear and experience. That whole John Travolta *Boy in the Plastic Bubble* idea looked very appealing to me. All of a sudden those homeschoolers I'd made fun of began to look a lot smarter. I considered whether or not I could spend my days wearing a denim jumper and making homemade granola while I taught Caroline from home.

(I'm totally kidding, by the way. I know not all homeschoolers wear denim jumpers.)

(Some of them wear denim skirts.)

(Seriously, I have a lot of friends who homeschool. I applaud their patience.)

After three years of sending Caroline to preschool two to three days a week, I thought I would feel more ready to send her off to kindergarten, but it felt so different. Preschool was kind and friendly. A safe little haven where she went to school with the kids of my closest friends in a cozy little church environment where they sang songs about Jesus and made flowerpot nativities every Christmas and had a special chapel celebration in honor of each student's birthday every year.

I knew the mean streets of public school weren't going to be nearly so nurturing and kind. We would have to get to know new kids and new families. My baby would be exposed to kids who might make fun of her lunch box or her sparkly tennis shoes, and I might be tempted to tackle someone who didn't even have permanent teeth yet.

I wanted Caroline to stay in the safe harbor of Christian preschool forever. In fact, the only reason I was even remotely happy about moving on was that it would mark the end of the annual creation of the Fiesta shoe-box float.

But as for everything else, it broke my heart to leave. On Caroline's last day of preschool I hugged the directors and thanked them for the way they had fiercely loved my child over the last three years, and I cried so hard I think I frightened them a little. I may have even begged them to consider starting a kindergarten.

Then came the night I was programming our DVR to record various shows throughout the week. At that moment it really dawned on me that I was about to send Caroline off to kindergarten. For the last five years, as our tastes graduated from *Sesame Street* to *Pinky Dinky Doo* to *Tom and Jerry*, the majority of our mornings had been spent snuggling on the couch watching TV together before we started our day. But now we were about to enter into the world of schedules and alarm clocks and extracurricular activities.

It's not like I didn't know it was coming. But there it was, looming big and bright on the horizon. And that's when something inside me began to ache more than a little. I wasn't ready to send my girl off to a big, wide world where she'd carry her own lunch tray and pick out what kind of milk she wanted. Of course, she doesn't even like milk, but that wasn't the point.

So I spent that summer dreading August. I didn't want school to start. I didn't want to send my baby to school, even though I tried to appear really excited every time we talked about it because I didn't want her to sense my fear. You know what they say about bees and dogs and five-year-olds.

About two weeks before school began, I was getting my hair cut, and my hairdresser asked me about Caroline—specifically how I disciplined Caroline when she acted up or did something wrong.

Here's what I said: "Lately I haven't had to discipline her that much. The year she was three was really hard because she tested me on everything, but now that she's five, I rarely have to discipline her. She knows I'm serious when I give her a look or get a certain tone in my voice, and she'll usually do whatever I've asked her to do."

Well, that was a mistake.

It was like I opened the vault of child-rearing fate and yelled, "This whole parenting thing is so easy! I have figured it all out!"

Don't ever do that. It's a big mistake.

Because the following two weeks were filled with more melt-downs and drama than an episode of *The Bachelor*.

At one point I put Caroline in time-out, and when I went in her room, I began to explain to her that Mama is the boss and she can't talk back to me. She looked at me and said, "If you say you're the boss one more time, I'm going to get myself so worked up that I don't know what I'll do." At which point I sent a flurry of prayers upward in the hope that God would sustain me for the next twenty years.

That's when I began to stare longingly at the calendar and count down the days until school started, because every day ended with my feeling tired and frustrated from fighting one battle after another all day long.

She was ready. I knew without a doubt that she was ready. It was evident in everything she did: from her fierce independence to the way she breezed through *Kindergarten Basics,* the workbook filled with exercises I'd bought for her. She was my social butterfly, and she was ready to fly.

And I had to let her.

Two weeks later I dressed her in a little pink sundress with a monogram on it and put in what would turn out to be one of the last bows she'd ever wear in her hair. We took a million pictures to document the moment, and then Perry and I drove her to school and began the long walk to her kindergarten classroom, each of us holding one of her little hands. Then suddenly she dropped our hands and said, "Follow me. I know where to go."

She walked ahead with her head held up and a backpack on her back that was almost bigger than she was. Oh, my heart. It was at that moment I realized I was going to have to let her lead the way to so many milestones.

We followed Caroline to her classroom, said hello to her teacher, and hugged Caroline good-bye. I managed to make it to the car before I began to cry in a way that would make Shirley MacLaine think I needed to quit being such a drama queen and get a grip. Perry and I prayed that God would watch over her and protect her and surround her with friends and his love. That's when the peace came in, because it was the reminder that God loved her even more than we did. He had big plans for her life, and kindergarten was just the beginning.

And you know what? She was just fine. And I was just fine. It was the beginning of a new adventure for both of us, and if you want to discover the new, you always have to leave the old behind. God can't take us anywhere if we keep clinging to little bits of the past. Which is a lesson I've had to learn at least once or a thousand times over the years.

∗

Kindergarten was great. Caroline and I both loved her teacher, and I was able to spend one day a week volunteering in her classroom or in the cafeteria, which is where I learned that five-year-olds are gross. And I also learned that there was at least one mom who felt the need to pack roll-your-own sushi in her child's lunch box. Way to make the rest of us feel guilty and mediocre with our offerings of peanut butter and honey on white bread, sister.

I believe it was in January of Caroline's kindergarten year that we got a note informing parents there would be an informational meeting for those of us interested in having our child tested for the gifted program. Which made me wonder what qualifies a kindergartner as gifted. They know to use a Kleenex instead of their finger? Or they don't try to eat the gold, spray-painted macaroni during craft time?

But I had to make a decision about whether or not to attend. I was torn because obviously Perry and I thought she was gifted. We knew she was gifted when she could pass gas like a man at only six months old, not to mention the fact she could spot a deer in the brush at 150 yards from the time she was three years old.

However, those qualities may not be exactly what Harvard is looking for, although they might be exactly what she needs to someday get her own hunting show on the Outdoor Channel.

But I wasn't sure I wanted to have Caroline labeled by the age of five. If she qualified for the gifted program, would it mean she'd feel too much pressure to perform academically? Would it take the joy out of school? I was much more concerned with raising a well-rounded person who enjoyed school than with being able to casually drop phrases in social settings about the struggles of raising a gifted child. "Oh, it was so difficult when we started trigonometry in second grade."

I thought about e-mailing Caroline's teacher to see if she thought we should have her tested. I figured she saw her in the classroom on a daily basis and probably had a better idea of what they were looking for to determine if a child was gifted. The problem was that I really liked Caroline's teacher and didn't want to send her a potentially awkward e-mail:

Dear Ms. Kindergarten Teacher,

You know that our precious baby girl, Caroline, is the light of our lives. We think she is the smartest, most well-adjusted child on the planet. She is able to leap tall buildings in a single bound, and we have no doubt she has a brilliant future as an Olympic athlete with a sideline career as the host of an incredibly successful reality television show or as a nuclear physicist. In other words, she has the potential to live the American dream.

We're sure you agree with us that there is no doubt she is gifted, but will you please let us know if you think she's not?

Sincerely and Totally Unbiased,
Perry and Melanie

See? Awkward.

Ultimately I decided to attend the meeting and see what they had to say because I didn't want to be the parent who says, "No way is my child gifted! I'm going to skip the meeting, stay home, and watch me some *Real Housewives of New York City* instead." I figured I needed to give Caroline a chance and not be defensive if someone dared to write on paper that my child wasn't intellectually superior to all the other kids in her class. At least I could rest in the knowledge she was smarter than the kid next to her who chewed the gum he found on the bottom of his desk.

When I walked in the door for the meeting, they gave me a handout. It was a checklist of behaviors, and I was supposed to check yes or no for each one. We were told this would be one of the determining factors for whether Caroline qualified for the program.

Apparently most of the parents in the room were gifted because they all realized pretty quickly that they'd better check yes to at least ten of the twelve characteristics or their child was getting sent straight to Doreen's Vocational School for Kids Who Can't Read So Good instead of spending a few hours a week discussing Einstein's theory of relativity with a bunch of other geniuses who didn't eat paste.

I sat in that meeting and realized I didn't want to assume Caroline wasn't gifted based on the fact that she came from a parent who consistently received report cards that read, "Does not live up to academic potential," which, translated, means, "Would rather flirt with cute boys and talk about who's having a party on Friday night while coming up with new ways to tease her bangs even higher."

(That would be me, by the way. Perry didn't flirt with boys, nor could he tease his bangs very high. Rumor has it that he did have a sweet mullet, though.)

But at the same time, I didn't really care one way or the other whether she was gifted or not. I just didn't want her to end up in therapy someday, saying, "It all started the day my mama decided I wasn't gifted when I was in kindergarten."

I quickly realized there were parents in the room who were taking the whole thing a lot more seriously than I was. This became clear when I whispered to a mom sitting next to me, "Well, if she's not gifted, it might just mean she'll be the prom queen instead." I promptly received what I feel certain was a dirty look.

Of course, in retrospect, maybe this woman had been the prom queen herself. And so it's safe to say that whether or not Caroline is gifted, we know for sure that I'm not gifted when it comes to social situations.

Ultimately, Caroline didn't make it into the gifted program that year, but one of her best friends did. Not that Caroline cared about that at all. It just fed my insecurities that maybe we should have done more flash cards instead of watching so many episodes of *The Backyardigans* because Tyrone the moose was so much more fun than learning phonics. But there was no way I couldn't feel a little concerned that Caroline's best friend would be reading aloud from Homer's *Odyssey* on the way to school every morning while Caroline sounded like Lloyd from *Dumb and Dumber* as she sounded out "t-t-t-h-uh" as she tried to read the word *the*.

I wish someone had told me then that children all learn at

their own pace and that reading is a developmental skill, just like everything else. Maybe someone did tell me that, but I was too neurotic to pay attention. I'm proud to say that today Caroline is now an excellent reader. And as it turned out, the gifted program in kindergarten was a three-month supplementary program where the kids learned about Egypt. Like you have to be gifted to do that? Here's a pyramid; here's King Tut; there was a woman named Cleopatra. The end.

Clearly I'm not one of those dragon mothers that you read about these days.

CHAPTER 19

The Big, Bad World of Elementary School

AFTER A SUCCESSFUL year of kindergarten we had to prepare (okay, mainly *I* had to prepare) for another big change. In our school district the kindergarten is its own little campus, and then the students move to a bigger school for first grade through fifth grade. Once again I had to let go of something that felt safe and secure. This seemed to be a theme God kept emphasizing in my life. *Comfort zone? Okay, let's keep moving forward.*

But the transition to first grade was practically seamless, with the exception of the first week, when I single-handedly created a car-pool traffic jam of epic proportions in my ignorance about which lane was the pick-up lane. Man, police officers can be so touchy.

So I decided I'd just walk in and pick Caroline up every

afternoon instead of navigating the tricky waters of the car pool. (See what I did there? Car pool? Waters? Now tell me who's gifted.)

Caroline's first grade teacher was young and enthusiastic. She taught the students their words and sounds using songs and rewarded them for good behavior by allowing them to make basketball shots in the classroom in a little plastic hoop on the back of the door. One day Caroline came home so excited she could barely speak as she told us her teacher had let the kids push her down the school ramps in her rolling desk chair. Now that's an educational experience.

Caroline quickly made new friends, and therefore I made new friends, and it was about as perfect as elementary school can be. Yes, the homework took some getting used to, and we had a few projects that brought out my inner crazy, such as creating a model of Christopher Columbus's ship, but the Fiesta float experience had given me practice for just such an occasion, and I'm happy to say Caroline and I did the whole thing without incident.

That was also the year Caroline really learned to read, and it brought me so much joy to see her pick up a book. Even though that didn't happen very often because, as she told me, "Why would I want to sit around and read a book when I could be out doing that stuff instead?" Yes, this is a child who comes from a dad who believes there is no finer reading than the latest Cabela's catalog. And even that grand tome is read only in the bathroom.

Classy.

$$*$$

Then it was time for second grade. And everything changed. When we got the letter about our teacher the week before school began, I was disappointed to see that Caroline had gotten the teacher everyone warned me about. But I tried to be positive and convince myself that our experience would be different. How could any teacher not like Caroline?

When I walked her to her classroom the first day of second grade, I had a pit in my stomach that wasn't helped at all by the stiff greeting we received when we met the teacher. I could tell immediately this wasn't going to be the warm, fuzzy experience we'd had for the past two years. And I could tell the teacher didn't think I was funny or charming at all.

It was a hard year. The teacher seemed to like Caroline well enough, but her teaching style was strict and no-nonsense, and this wasn't helped by the fact that she had a class full of behavior problems. I watched as Caroline went from a happy-go-lucky kid who was excited to go to school every morning to a little girl who bit her nails and scratched her head in nervousness and wanted to stay home in the mornings. It broke my heart.

And so I prayed. I prayed for wisdom and guidance and discernment. Should I homeschool? Should we move her to private school? Was I supposed to go get belligerent with the school staff and demand that my child be switched to another classroom? Because those were the things I wanted to do.

But I felt God clearly telling me that I needed only to be still and trust him. So that's what I did. Perry and I did our best to encourage Caroline and let her know she was in that class for a reason. Her job was to let her light shine brightly and to know that we were always on her side. But it wasn't easy.

I realize that school isn't always going to be fun, but second grade seems awfully early to have to learn that life lesson.

Yet it was the reality. Which was why I was so surprised when Caroline got in the car one Friday afternoon full of excitement and told me that her teacher said she had a "huge surprise" for the class on Monday. This seemed completely out of character but, sure enough, I got home and discovered the teacher had sent out an e-mail to the parents informing us the kids were getting a "huge surprise" on Monday.

All weekend long Caroline speculated about what the huge surprise could possibly be. An ice cream party? Maybe a dance party, complete with a disco ball? A pet guinea pig for the class?

On Monday morning Caroline jumped out of bed, beside herself at the prospect that the unveiling of the huge surprise was imminent. I dropped her off and told her I couldn't wait to hear all about it when I picked her up that afternoon.

As soon as she hopped in the car at the end of the day, I asked, "What was it? What was the huge surprise?" She looked at me with an expression of pure and total disgust on her face as she announced in a monotone voice, "Tim Duncan's shoe."

"What did you say?" I asked, thinking I had surely heard wrong or missed a piece of the story.

"I said it was Tim Duncan's shoe," she repeated with absolutely no enthusiasm.

"His shoe?"

"Yes. Tim Duncan's shoe."

For those of you who may not know, Tim Duncan is a basketball player for the San Antonio Spurs. Like most basketball players, he is tall, and I'd estimate that his shoe size is probably around a 14. Caroline's teacher had written to Tim Duncan and requested that he send her an autographed shoe. Apparently she thought the kids in the class might be motivated to have good behavior if they had the promise of getting to keep Tim Duncan's shoe on their desk as a reward. So technically, yes, that is a "huge surprise." But I will tell you that Caroline and I learned an important lesson that day: there is a big difference between a huge surprise and a fun surprise.

The biggest question in my mind was how anyone could think an enormous shoe would inspire a bunch of seven-year-olds who had spent the weekend dreaming of eating ice cream and dancing under a disco ball. Don't ever promise kids a huge surprise that doesn't involve the opportunity for total chaos. It doesn't translate.

Perry and I immediately adopted the phrase "Tim Duncan's shoe" as code for anything we deemed boring and lame. It has proved to be terribly useful. Invited to a boring charity dinner? Tim Duncan's shoe. Sitting through a PTO meeting? Tim Duncan's shoe. Listening to our neighbor rant about politics? Tim Duncan's shoe.

So I guess the bottom line is that while elementary school hasn't always proved to be fun and has presented its share of challenges, I can't say we all aren't learning a few pieces of valuable information.

School is the beginning of the real world, the end of the protective bubble. It's a time to learn that not everyone uses their nice words, a time to learn that you'll run out of jackets if you keep leaving them on the playground, a time to learn that there are sometimes battles you have to fight. There are highs and lows and struggles and triumphs.

And there are days that sometimes feel like Tim Duncan's shoe.

CHAPTER 20

It's a Party
& I'll Cry If I Want To

I NEVER HAD a piñata at any of my birthday parties. Of course I realize now that is probably grounds for some kind of therapy, but I was a child of the '70s, and we didn't know about such things. A birthday party was a small affair with a homemade cake, ice cream, and if you were really lucky, some balloons. There were no piñatas in those days. No treat bags to say thanks for coming. If you had asked for a party favor back then, you might have been met with, "You know what you can take with you, kid? The memory of some good cake."

Did I mention we also had to walk uphill BOTH WAYS in the snow to attend most of these parties?

Or maybe everyone else was having great parties and I just never knew about it because I wasn't invited. If that's the case, please don't tell me because I visit the edge enough as it is.

I certainly don't need to know there were extravaganzas happening all around me complete with fancy bakery cakes.

My birthday is in August. Also known as the Tim Duncan's shoe of birthday months because it's summer, it's hot, and all your friends are probably on vacation. So the majority of my birthdays were spent either at the pool or at Six Flags with whatever friends had the misfortune of being born into a family that didn't take vacations.

And that was totally fine until September, when the first kid in my class would have a birthday and his mom would walk in with cupcakes and I'd be reminded of the fact that I'd been born in the worst month.

Given this childhood trauma, I was a little disappointed when I realized my due date with Caroline fell smack dab in the middle of August. I had inadvertently passed the bad birthday gene to my offspring, who would suffer her mother's fate of having party options that consisted of (1) having a pool party, (2) having a pool party, or (3) inviting people over to sit on a block of ice.

What I didn't realize then was that the time of year would be the least of my worries. I wasn't prepared for this whole new world of birthday party competition.

The first time I remember having full-on birthday party envy was in seventh grade. Jamie Hornbeck had a dance party in her garage, complete with a DJ. There was a table set up with a bowl of cheese puffs and some Dr Pepper. And a disco ball. Be still, my heart. To this day it might be the best party I've ever attended. That garage turned into a place of pure awesomeness under the dim lights and with the sweet sounds of Journey singing "Faithfully" while we all slow-danced awkwardly in our Jordache jeans and jelly shoes.

But times are different now. Birthday parties have become a new competitive sport. I can't remember exactly when I first became aware of this, but I think it was somewhere around the time Gulley took Jackson to a one-year-old's birthday party and called me on the way home to inform me it was nicer than her wedding reception. And her wedding reception was very nice.

She said, "They had even planted new flowers in the front beds to match the decor. There were LINEN tablecloths. There were silver chafing dishes and margarita machines."

I was stunned into temporary silence until I managed to utter, "Really?"

"YES," she replied. "I wanted to live there forever."

You would think that a sane person planning a birthday party might think linen tablecloths and silver chafing dishes are a little much to honor a birthday boy who might take a nap during the entire party and drool on himself. Of course I know some people who may have spent their twenty-first birthdays in a similar fashion, but that's not the point.

Anyway, I made a point about the whole thing just seeming like a ridiculous waste of time and money since I like to climb on the occasional soapbox concerning topics I think won't ever apply to me. And so I made sure that Caroline's first several birthday parties were modest affairs. Yes, we had bakery cakes, but that had more to do with my limited baking abilities than a need to impress. For the most part, though, these were small gatherings at home with a handful of family and some little toddler friends. There may have been some bubbles or sidewalk chalk as a parting gift.

But then came Caroline's sixth birthday.

Otherwise known as my own personal cautionary tale about excess and overdoing things.

*

That year Caroline announced that she wanted to have four friends spend the night. And I welled up with memories of slumber parties and giggling girlfriends and sleeping with our sleeping bags all bunched together as we whispered well into the night.

My baby's first slumber party. It was like a full-circle moment.

I agreed to the slumber party, and then she suggested it might be fun to also have a big pool party that same day so she could celebrate with all her friends before the smaller gathering in the evening. Maybe it was the guilt over passing down the lame birthday month to my daughter, or maybe it was the heat, or maybe she just caught me in a really good mood. Whatever the reason, something false in me whispered, "How hard could that be? It's just a pool party!" And I agreed to it.

Do not ever let yourself be suckered into such a thing.

Because I essentially agreed to plan and perform two birthday parties in one day. The pool party became an exercise in stress as I searched for cute invitations to mail out to her friends, a cake that would serve thirty kids, coordinating plates and streamers to decorate the cabana at the pool, and a giant unicorn piñata.

Oh, that's right. Not just any piñata. A giant unicorn.

Fortunately, Gulley's husband, Jon, works on the south side of San Antonio, where they sell piñatas on the side of the road on a daily basis. I commissioned him to buy me the largest unicorn piñata he could find. And if he couldn't find a unicorn, then a horse would do. I could always make a horn with my legendary piñata-making skills.

Or my ability to get creative with an empty paper towel roll and some tissue paper.

Whatever.

I knew Jon had taken me seriously when he called to let me know he'd found a white unicorn and was just trying to figure out how to fit it in his car. He drives an SUV.

Through sheer will and possibly bending one of the papier-mâché unicorn legs, he was able to deliver the unicorn to my house. Perry and I promptly christened it Unicorn Gigante while Caroline fell head over heels in love with it and spent the two days prior to the party sitting on it like it was a brand-new pet pony. Honestly, I wasn't sure if she was going to be able to demolish him with a stick when the big day came.

But I underestimated her. When I questioned whether she was ready to fill the unicorn with candy, she looked at me and said, "He is GOING DOWN." And so I dissected him from the top to fill him full of candy, figuring we could always take out a second mortgage. We stuffed him full of Nerds and Dum Dum suckers and taped him back up.

When I tried to move him to the back door, I realized he now weighed approximately seventy-eight pounds. I lifted a silent prayer to heaven that the rope would hold him, because nothing ruins a party mood faster than a gigantic unicorn hurtling to the earth and frightening small children.

Perry came home to help me get everything ready for the

party, and I informed him that Gigante was pretty solid. In fact, I was worried the party guests might not be able to break him open despite repeated beatings. So Perry took a butcher knife and stabbed Gigante a few times in the chest just to weaken him a little bit.

It was just like that scene in *Gladiator* when Joaquin Phoenix stabs Russell Crowe with that knife before they go out into the Colosseum to ensure that he wins the fight.

Except we were going to a party for our six-year-old at the pool.

And it wasn't really that dramatic.

The Roman Empire wasn't at stake or anything.

By the time we arrived at the pool to set up the party, I was already exhausted. And way past wondering why I ever thought it was a good idea to host this large party and then a sleepover.

The partygoers all arrived and ate bowls of Goldfish crackers, drank their weight in lemonade, and swam until it was time for cake. Sadly, I spent much of this time treading water in the deep end with only a pool noodle to support me because some of the party guests were questionable swimmers and yet their own mothers didn't feel the need to wear a bathing suit to the pool. Not that I was bitter about it. I'm always super happy to have your kid jump on my head repeatedly. Good times.

Finally it was time to eat the mermaid birthday cake and to beat the heck out of Gigante. And he held up amazingly well. In fact, when all was said and done, only his leg broke, allowing the candy to spill out with some help from Perry, who was shaking him vigorously to speed up the process.

And then it was all over. But not really, because I still had to entertain five little girls for the rest of the night. Little girls who finished all the crafts I'd bought to entertain them inside of thirty minutes and quickly demanded that I give them all pedicures.

Which I was happy to do until they realized they liked each other's color selections better than their own and asked me to redo them. At this point I'd been partying for close to twelve hours. I couldn't do that in college and certainly not when I'm staring down my late thirties. It was time to call it a night.

I helped the girls settle into their sleeping bags and put in a movie in the hope that it would calm them down and let them drift off to sleep so I could stagger off to my own bed and collapse.

But I quickly realized why all my friends' mothers were so grumpy when we were growing up. It was the slumber parties. We drove them to it. Most days Mrs. Jones probably didn't walk around with a scowl on her face while growling, "GO TO SLEEP. RIGHT. NOW." She was most likely a perfectly wonderful woman with a sweet disposition. It was all our giggling and our refusal to use inside voices that turned her mean.

Because somewhere around 1:00 a.m. I began to channel Miss Hannigan from *Annie*. I was no longer kind and friendly. I came out in my robe, my hair disheveled, making threats like, "IF YOU DON'T GO TO BED RIGHT NOW, I'M TAKING YOU ALL HOME." I was seconds away from telling the girls I was going to make them mop my kitchen floor until it shone like the top of the Chrysler building when they, mercifully, passed out from sheer exhaustion.

And then I did the same. Vowing to myself that I would never, ever be this stupid again.

At least until the next year.

CHAPTER 21

One Isn't Always
the Loneliest Number

I'LL TELL YOU something not many people know about me.

I'm pretty sure I invented Facebook.

Oh, sure, you may be thinking you don't remember seeing my name in the movie *Social Network* or hearing me mentioned in media reports about Mark Zuckerberg. And you're right. I've never gotten so much as a mention. Yet I know for a fact that I came up with the basic premise for social media as a whole back in 1999, when I was preparing to attend my ten-year high school reunion.

As I tried on various outfits looking for just the right thing to make me look both impossibly thin and like I wasn't trying too hard, I commented to Gulley that I didn't really care anything about making small talk with a bunch of people I largely hadn't seen in ten years, but I wished there was a way to just see a recent picture of them with a few paragraphs about who they married, what they do for a living, if they have kids, and if they ended up serving any time.

(If you were in my graduating class and are reading this book, I'm not referring to you. I loved catching up with you and making small talk at our ten-year reunion. I'm just talking about other people. People who don't feel the need to buy a book written by one of their high school classmates.)

But I don't let my bitterness over not receiving any billions or even tens of dollars from my invention keep me from getting on Facebook and looking around on a regular (maybe hourly) basis, because I am nosy and I love to see what people have done with their lives. Especially the people I grew up with, since we all change and grow, and life has a way of turning out so much different from what we imagined when we were sixteen and thought we might be the next Jane Pauley, until we walked into our first communications class in college and had a cynical, bitter professor tell us that we had a better chance of becoming president of the United States than ending up on network news.

Nice. Dream killer.

Way to shape the minds and hearts of the youth of America.

Anyway, the only problem with social media is that now we know so much about people we haven't seen in a sweet forever. And then if we actually see them in person (like at a reunion), there isn't much ground left for small talk. We already know where they live, who they married, and if they like to post pictures of themselves in swimsuits to show off the results of their low-carb diet. And so what do you talk about? Real stuff? The fact that you drive a Dodge Stratus and the most exciting thing that happened to you in recent months was a good report from the dentist? Doubtful.

If you're me, then you just smile and feel awkward for a few minutes before claiming that you need to go refresh your drink or get another plate of sausage balls. But, then again, my social skills are legendary.

So I guess it's partly because of social media that I assume most of my old friends already know Caroline is an only child and why I'm taken aback when an acquaintance gives me a questioning look of pity/disapproval when I tell them I have one child.

A few months ago I was at a tailgate party and Gulley introduced me to one of her husband's college friends. We made small talk (my favorite!), and he eventually asked me what I did for a living. I never admit I'm a writer because it feels weird and kind of pretentious and makes me sound smarter than I really am.

(Not to mention people automatically assume you spend all day in your pajamas.)

(Rightfully so.)

I mumbled something about being "just a mom."

That's when Gulley piped in. "She's a writer. She's writing her first book."

Naturally I glared at her for exposing my secret while he asked, "What's your book about?"

I responded, "Motherhood."

And that's when he hit me with, "Well, you need to have more than one kid to write a book about motherhood."

I really hope the bruise from where I kicked him healed okay. Because maybe I'm defensive about the whole thing.

(Yes. A little.)

(Or a lot, depending on the day.)

But who decided you have to have more than one child to make you a real mother? I don't know many women who didn't have their whole world turn upside down like a snow globe that sprinkles love, compassion, and ferocity beyond their wildest dreams the moment their first baby was placed in their arms. So maybe I'm biased, but I believe that's when a mama is made. And I'm sure if there are two or three or six more who come after that, then the feeling is the same each time. Even if you're too tired to fully appreciate it.

Maybe my days aren't filled with coordinating schedules and sports and homework for more than one little person, but my heart is full with my one child. And to be honest, I struggled with our decision to have one child for a long time. This may be partly due to the fact my mother-in-law predicted we'd only have one, and I desperately wanted to prove her wrong. Wow. That sounds even pettier typed out than it does in my head, but it's the truth, so I'm leaving it there for all the world to see.

✳

I'm assuming Perry and I could have had another child if we'd tried again, and I want to be transparent about that since so many women struggle with infertility even after being able to have a child. This was an intentional decision we made based on a lot of prayer and second-guessing and my getting over a preconceived notion that a "real family" needs to have at least two kids. Preferably a boy and a girl. A set of kids. Like salt and pepper shakers.

There was a time after Caroline started kindergarten when I really thought I might want to try to have another baby. Perry and I talked about it, and he made it clear he was happy with our family the way it was, but we agreed we'd pray about it and see what happened. I was convinced God would change Perry's heart on the matter, and I began to envision how I'd decorate a new nursery.

But as it turned out, my heart was the one that began to change. And I didn't go down easily. I cried over the surrender of the family I'd always envisioned in my head and had to come to a place where I realized God had other plans for us. Truthfully, part of me felt like a failure and wondered why I wasn't one of those women who could raise six kids and home-school all of them and serve milk and cookies every afternoon in some clever way like all the moms on Pinterest do.

I had to come to terms with the fact that, while I have other strengths, being a mom to a bunch of kids may not be my gift considering I don't really handle chaos or messes well and have been known to hide in the closet to let my inner introvert take deep, cleansing breaths. I had to face who I really am and what I'm equipped to do versus the person I sometimes like to fantasize I am. It's like the internal struggle I have between wanting to give away all my money to feed hungry children and wanting to buy a Louis Vuitton bag. I'd like to believe I'm not shallow enough to care about things like fine handbags, but the truth is I kind of do. And like Gulley says, at least when you're wading in the shallow end of life, you don't have to worry about getting your expensive purse wet.

But I came to a point of contentment and peace about Caroline being our only child and realized we were already a tightly knit little band of three. We were complete.

And that's not to say that there still aren't days that I long to hold another baby in my arms. In fact, there are some days I still wonder if God might have something or someone else for us, even as I hear my biological clock ticking loudly.

(Loudly.)

(At times it seems to scream, "You're forty, sister.")

(The train is about to leave the station.)

But I think that's part of being a mother. Once you've held a child who belongs to you in your arms and kissed little chubby legs and laughed at those bracelets of fat and had a little person hold your face in her hands and say, "I love you, Mama," do you ever really get over the feeling that you'd like to do it one more time? I mean, sure, I can get myself some kind of fluffy little dog to dress up and carry around in a purse instead, but it's not really the same.

So I guess what I'm saying is I don't know that I'll ever be able to put a definite punctuation on the sentence that is our family, but right now it feels like a period. No pun intended.

I rest in knowing that God couldn't have chosen a child who better fits our family. How many girls think the perfect Christmas is getting her very own pistol and holster and a pair of glittery gold TOMS? She's the perfect blend of the two of us. To quote the great Donny and Marie Osmond, she's "a little bit country" and "a little bit rock and roll."

And so maybe the next time I update my status on Facebook, I'll write, "Yes, we only have one child. But we think we got the best one." Then people will probably unfriend me because I'm obnoxious, and they won't even care that I'm the one who invented the whole thing in the first place.

CHAPTER 22

Brothers
from Another Mother

ONE OF THE (stupid) questions people ask about having an only child is if I'm worried she'll be spoiled. Because no one has ever known a family with three kids who are all totally rotten. And my answer is no. Sure, we may be able to give Caroline a little bit more than we could if she had siblings, but we aren't allowing her to grow up with a sense of entitlement.

I will not stand for a Veruca Salt in my house. I am not afraid to say no—loudly and often. And I tend to say it loudest these days when we walk by Justice, because that is an array of some tacky merchandise perfectly designed to entice little girls with all the sparkles and the hot-pink animal prints.

God has given my family one of the greatest gifts any person can have, whether we come from a family of three or twenty—friends who have become family. Gulley's boys give Caroline all the benefits and angst that siblings provide for each other, because no child should have to grow up not knowing what it is to fight for her space in the backseat of the car.

Jackson and Will are the closest things to brothers she could have without my actually giving birth to two boys. And best of all, Perry and I don't have to worry about how we'll keep two large boys fed during their teen years or how we'll pay for their college. Total score.

Sometimes the best families are the ones God builds using unexpected pieces of our hearts. Or like I read one time, "Friends are God's way of apologizing for your relatives."

$$*$$

When we met more than twenty years ago, I couldn't have imagined that someday Gulley and I would live a mile away from each other, that we'd take road trips with our kids, and that they would love each other as much as we love each other. But they do. To this day, when we ask them who they want to play with, they always request each other before anyone else.

Gulley's older son, Jackson, was eighteen months old when Caroline was born. And I insisted that Gulley bring him over to meet her by the time she was a week old. Gulley walked in the door carrying Jackson, who'd been our baby up until that time, and all of a sudden he looked enormous. When did his hands get so big? Was that facial hair? What happened to the red-haired baby?

He'd been replaced by a new baby. He was the big kid now. I have the sweetest picture of Gulley holding him while he peeked over the edge of Caroline's crib and saw her for the first time. I like to think it was love at first sight even though it was probably at least a year before he really appreciated her. It's hard to be enthusiastic about something that just poops and cries—at least when you're a toddler. Or a thirty-two-year-old.

Jackson and Caroline were already best buddies by the time Will came along, thanks to the countless hours they'd spent together in Gulley's backyard while their mamas discussed everything from sleepless nights to potty training to our thoughts on wedge heels.

But Jackson and Caroline embraced Will. He became "Brother," and they babied him endlessly. Finally Caroline had someone she could boss around, even though Will isn't really a fellow who likes to be told what he can and cannot do. He once told me when he was just two years old that he was "gonna bust somebody's tail" if the outdoor playground at McDonald's wasn't open that day.

When they all were little, Caroline and I would go over to Gulley's house almost every afternoon, and the three of them would pile into Jackson's battery-operated red Jeep and take turns playing chauffeur. We watched over the years as they were no longer entertained by just driving each other around and instead started seeing who could hold onto the hood of the Jeep the longest while the driver sped through the yard at full speed and Gulley and I yelled out threats and admonitions about the potential for a trip to the emergency room.

Gulley and I have a term we use to describe docile, gentle children. We call them "cup pourers." The name is derived from the little kids who sit on the edge of the baby pool in the summertime and are perfectly content to just fill their little nesting cups with water and then dump them out and then fill their cups and dump them out while their mamas get to engage in enjoyable adult conversation and never have to make the run of shame around the pool in their bathing suits to chase a toddler who has decided to break free from the bonds of the baby pool in search of deeper waters.

I tried desperately to make Caroline a cup pourer. I even bought her this fabulous plastic Cinderella tea set to take to the pool in the hope it would entice her to sit for hours and "make tea" in the baby pool. (As opposed to making "tee," which is another favorite pastime of the toddler crowd.) But despite all our best efforts, Gulley and I did not give birth to cup pourers. We have three kids who are constantly on the lookout for the party, any party. As long as there is fun to be had or the potential to give your mother a heart attack, they're in.

And so our constant refrains over the years are "You're going to end up in the hospital!" and "Why did you kick him?" and "Didn't we JUST SAY that you couldn't play in the mud?" Followed closely by "Y'all need to work it out. We all LOVE each other."

Because while Jackson tends to be the peacemaker of the gang, Will and Caroline are like fire and ice. We've always maintained that we will never allow them to date because none of us could survive the drama. They are either totally in love with each other or threatening each other with cries of "I'm going to lock you in this room if you try to tell on me." Of course Perry once made the comment that it sounds like a typical marriage to him. He's hilarious.

Just a few weeks ago we were all at the Little League fields watching Jackson play baseball. Actually, Gulley and I were watching him play baseball. Caroline and Will were engaging in their favorite ballpark activity, which is seeing how much money they can spend at the concession stand. All of a sudden the two of them came running up to us, and it was easy to tell there was some sort of argument going on.

Apparently Caroline had bought some blue Sour Punch Straws and then realized she had to go to the bathroom. So she asked Will to hold them while she ran in the restroom, and by the time she came out, he had "lost" them. Which I think we all know is code for "I shoved them all in my mouth and didn't think about the ramifications."

Caroline told me her side of the story while Will told Gulley his side. And I think Gulley and I both knew exactly what happened, but we pleaded the case of each other's child to our own. I said, "He might have lost them. Maybe he set them down somewhere and someone picked them up. Why don't you just go buy some more?"

Meanwhile, I heard Gulley questioning, "Did you eat her blue Sour Punch Straws? Did you? Be honest."

And he looked her straight in the eye and said, "Please believe me, Mom. I didn't eat them. I DIDN'T."

So we told them they needed to let it go and get along. Caroline ran off to buy another round of Sour Punch Straws, and Will tagged along behind her. Gulley turned to me and said, "I'm almost positive my child just lied to my face and has no soul today, but I can't prove he ate them, even though I'm 98 percent sure he did."

It was the perfect crime.

But Caroline and Will worked it out and came back with a

new pack of Sour Punch Straws that they shared as they watched Jackson pitch, and they cheered loudly when he struck out two batters in a row. Then they begged us to let them all go home together because we had NO IDEA how much they missed each other. Even though they'd just spent two hours hanging out and fighting and making up. Like a two-hour special episode of *Real Housewives of Whatever City*.

Because, at the end of the day, they always love each other.

When they're all together, they take on their respective roles. Jackson is the protective big brother. He once stared down a little boy who had been giving Caroline a hard time at school, telling Gulley, "That boy is bad news." I'm counting on him to get her safely through high school. Caroline becomes the middle child, always searching for a way to make everyone laugh so she can bask in the center of attention. Which has unfortunately resulted in some mooning incidents. And Will is the baby. On the lookout to make sure he isn't being wronged in some way, sometimes getting left out, but ultimately always adored.

Jackson and Will have taught Caroline what it's like to have brothers. Together, they love and they laugh. They wrestle and they fight. They argue over who gets the biggest cupcake, and they roll their eyes at their mothers when they think we're not paying attention or saying something they deem to be totally embarrassing.

And in return, I believe Caroline has taught the boys that having a sister means there is always a good chance for tears and drama, even when you're not sure what you did wrong. And that having a girl around makes your world a little bit sweeter.

Even if it's a girl who can burp as loud as you.

CHAPTER 23

Like a Band of Idiots We Go down the Highway

EVERY MOTHER KNOWS the reason Robert Frost took the road less traveled is because he wasn't traveling with children who needed to go to the bathroom every thirty minutes. Otherwise he would have taken the road paved with McDonald's and truck stops with restrooms, covered by antibacterial hand soap and prayer. And *that* would have made all the difference.

There is no other experience that can bring a family together like hours spent in the car wondering if the person next to you is going to get carsick again. Ultimately the road trip is much like the actual parenting journey: it takes you to new, unexpected places while you marvel that you just had to ask the question, "Why are you licking the bottom of your brother's shoe?" or "Do you need to throw up in this plastic cup again?"

Of course, we don't take the normal family road trip where

Mom and Dad load up the Griswold family Truckster and hit the open road. Mainly because Perry isn't a big fan of traveling unless it involves making the forty-five-minute trek to the ranch to shoot something. And that doesn't count as a road trip in my mind because there's barely enough time in the car to have a reason to stop and buy some Corn Nuts and a Diet Coke at a sketchy gas station that makes you feel like you might be taking your life into your own hands. Not to mention the trip ends when all you can see is cactus.

The fortunate thing is that Gulley's husband, Jon, isn't really up for the road trip experience either. At least not the way we do it. Gulley has actually called me after they've returned from a trip to complain that Jon didn't even want to stop for a bucket of fried chicken. And at that point you have to ask, "What's the point of even getting in the car?" Why not just take a plane and pay six dollars for a bag of trail mix and a quarter cup of Diet Coke and be done with it?

So, as with most things in life, Gulley and I have discovered we are road trip soul mates. We believe in the importance of a good playlist, frequent stops for snacks and/or a bucket of fried chicken, and seeing the sights along the way because you may get only one chance in life to see an actual snake farm. (I still haven't recovered.)

Our first road trip together with the kids was about the time Will was a little over a year old, Caroline wasn't quite three, and Jackson was four. We loaded up Gulley's SUV, strapped the kids in their car seats, sprinkled ourselves with holy water, and headed to see her parents. Mainly because we knew her mom would feed us good food and help us with the kids, and it was the closest thing to a real vacation we could think of since Perry and Jon shot down our suggestion that we fly to Cozumel for a week while they kept the kids.

I think we were about thirty minutes into the drive when Will began to cry because he still had to sit in a rear-facing car seat and wasn't one bit happy about it. And then Caroline began to cry because Will was crying and it hurt her ears. And then Jackson began to cry because it was like that moment on a turbulent flight when you notice the flight attendants have put up the drink cart and are beginning to quietly panic. That's when we discovered that Gulley is extremely dexterous as she maneuvered back and forth between the front and the backseat, trying to keep everyone happy while I continued to drive, looking for a place to stop and buy some Xanax from someone on the street.

But when we finally arrived at our destination, we were all happy to be there and thrilled to be together for three days in a row. So a tradition was born. We decided right then and there that we would load up the kids and ourselves for a week every summer to take a tour of Texas, stopping at various locations and attractions along the way before reaching our final destination. (By final destination, I mean Gulley's parents' house in Bryan, Texas, not heaven. Even though there have been times we thought the trip might kill us.)

✳

Gulley grew up in Bryan/College Station, home of my alma mater, Texas A&M University. I grew up in Houston and later Beaumont, Texas, but my mom moved to Oklahoma during my freshman year of college. My dad and my stepmom lived in Houston, but I needed a closer place to occasionally take a break from the dorm.

So once Gulley and I became friends in college, I began spending so much time at her parents' house that I was pretty much adopted into her family. Or maybe I just kept hanging out there until they had to come to terms with the fact they couldn't get rid of me. Because you know what college kids love more than just about anything? Besides cheap beer? A place to eat a delicious, home-cooked meal, and a washer and dryer where you can do your laundry without stockpiling quarters for weeks on end.

In fact, there may have even been a summer when I just moved into her parents' house because it seemed to make more sense than driving over there every single day. And I think it speaks volumes about what kind of people they are because they let me. And they fed me. They took me in and made me their own.

Maybe the whole thing was a little like the movie *What about Bob?* But I choose to not examine that too closely.

A large part of the fun is that Gulley's entire family is a cast of characters, and I love them for it. The matriarch is Gulley's grandmother, Nena. Nena is the quintessential Southern belle, and she will be quick to tell you, "I subscribe to *Vogue* and *Harper's Bazaar* to keep up with all the latest fashions." She wore a poncho and embroidered jeans to Jackson's birthday party a few years ago, and she looked so good that Granddaddy (her husband of sixty years, who is suffering from a little bit of memory loss) introduced himself to her at the party and said he'd like to take her out and get to know her better.

One of my favorite Nena memories is the Thanksgiving she invited my then-boyfriend and me to dinner. When I was in school, Texas A&M and the University of Texas (UT) always played on Thanksgiving Day, so everyone stayed in town instead of going home for the holiday.

We showed up with the requested relish tray (I wasn't even sure what that was), and she immediately told my boyfriend, "Oh, I just love your sweater! If you ever decide to sell that at a garage sale, you let me know." Gulley was mortified, but I was hysterical. Later on Nena told us she didn't know what else to say because "that boy was so good looking, if he had asked me to run away with him, I would've said, 'Hold on, let me get my purse!'" Because a good Southern Baptist woman may decide to run away from home, but she'd never leave her purse behind. What if she needed six tissues, some breath mints, and eighteen tubes of lipstick in an array of colors?

One night when I was at Gulley's house, I ended up sitting next to Nena, and she revealed that she was in the market for a new car. She didn't really know what make or model, but she was insistent that it must have a sunroof. I sat there thinking how chick (as Nena's best friend pronounces the word *chic*) Nena was to want a car with a sunroof at eighty-seven years old and envisioning her driving to the Winn-Dixie with the wind in her hair.

Then she said, "Yes, I must have a sunroof because on the news they always show people caught in floodwaters escaping through the sunroof. I need a sunroof so I can get out of the car if I'm caught in a flood." (No, I haven't seen a news clip of anyone being rescued through their sunroof either.)

I asked the question that was on everyone's mind. "Nena, do you even drive when it's raining?" I felt fairly certain I knew the answer.

"Well . . . no. But you just never know." Uncle Johnny chomped on his cigar and said, "Well, Mama, just make sure if you're ever caught in rising water, you open that sunroof before the water gets too high, because otherwise it's not going to work any better than the windows, and then you've wasted good money on a sunroof."

Later on Uncle Johnny pulled me aside. "I hate to think about Mama getting caught in a flood," he said, "but I'd pay good money to see her try to get through a sunroof." Which completely summed up my feelings on the matter.

Eventually the conversation turned from how to survive a flood to religious matters. Nena told us about her search for a new television. She said she went into Circuit City and told them she needed the biggest and best TV money could buy and money was NO OBJECT because her TV is as dear to her as her Bible.

And while we were on the subject of religion, Uncle Glen told us about his church. Uncle Glen lives in a solar-paneled log cabin in a little town outside of Bryan, and as Gulley's mama will tell you, he was always a little different. Nena thought it was because she cried so hard when she found out she was pregnant with him.

But anyway, it seems that the church he attended used to be Church of Christ, but membership kept declining so "they wheeled in a piano and an organ and changed the sign outside to say nondenominational, and now we're up to 130 members."

And they were serious about the nondenominational part because during Communion they put wine in the inner circle of the tray, along with grape juice for the former Baptists who still preferred to drink in the privacy of their own closets.

The only flaw in the new, improved nondenominational church was that they discovered that their preacher, after eight years of marrying and burying various members of the congregation, wasn't licensed or ordained. There might be some folks living in sin despite the best of intentions.

But I'm sure it's some consolation that they had lovely organ music during the ceremony.

If everyone had an adoptive extended family like that, I am convinced Disney World would go bankrupt. Because in a day when everyone feels like you have to sell the family farm to get your kids to the Magic Kingdom by the age of two, I believe it's about the simple things in life. Good friends, family, junk food, and yelling, "Don't make me have to pull over!"

I want my daughter to grow up with an appreciation for the open road and touring the state capital in Austin or stopping in Waco just so the kids can see the Baylor Bear or driving to Dallas to ride the city metro bus and take our lives in our own hands.

An old-fashioned road trip offers a little bit of pure Americana that can get lost in this fast-paced world where we feel like we need to compete with the Joneses. I guarantee our kids have had as much or more fun on our little adventures than some poor kid who has been subjected to the "We are going to have fun if it kills us because this cost us a fortune" mentality that more exotic trips can bring.

*

Normally it's about a three-hour drive from San Antonio to College Station—if you make the drive without any children in the car. For us, it takes about the same amount of time it took the Ingalls family to make it across the Midwestern plains in the dead of winter as they fought wolves, Indians, and the bitter cold.

Usually at the halfway point we stop at McDonald's so the kids can use the bathroom and order a Happy Meal to get the free toy and eat half a Chicken McNugget and four paper cups filled with ketchup.

But Gulley and I often feel we can't stomach another meal at McDonald's. We are grown women. We need something a little more sophisticated, a little more refined.

So we make a run for the border.

Which for us is a true delicacy because Taco Bells are next to nonexistent when you live in San Antonio, Texas—home to over 852 Mexican restaurants.

In spite of the easy access to some of the best Mexican food in the world, Gulley and I still crave Taco Bell from time to time. Which just goes to show, you can take the girls out of East Texas, but you can't take East Texas out of the girls.

This stop is also our chance to load up on Diet Coke to fortify us for the remainder of the trip because by this point we're usually beginning to question our sanity and wonder how one child can ask, "Are we there yet?" at five-second intervals.

The kids never disappoint us in that regard. Usually we're in the car only about four minutes before one of them asks, "How much longer until we get there?"

I reply, "We'll get there when we get there. Don't ask us that every five minutes."

"Okay . . . but how much longer till we get there?"

The good news is they only ask about forty-two more times over the course of three hours. And in between they alternate which two of them are going to annoy the other one until that one decides to tell on the other two. Then they interrupt Gulley and me to rat out their fellow man. What they don't know is that Gulley and I decided a long time ago we would have a strict policy of telling them, "Work it out yourselves," because we're too busy discussing wrinkle creams and our hair to get involved in their backseat drama.

✳

After one of our visits to Bryan it was about time to head home, but Gulley and I weren't in any hurry to get on the road, so we decided to take the kids to a nearby splash pad to burn some energy before we got in the car. Will decided he'd rather go with Honey, which is what the kids call Gulley's mama, to visit Nena because Nena styles his hair for him when he visits and he's a fan of the gelled coiffure. So Gulley and I took Caroline and Jackson to play in the water, which was a great idea until Caroline fell and skinned her knee and the top of her foot.

You would have thought we'd just amputated her leg with a dull butter knife. She was actually fine until she saw the blood, and then she got the vapors. We left the park to pick up Chick-fil-A for lunch while Caroline continued to moan about her injury and the cruelty of life. It was like a monologue from a Lifetime movie and finally ended with my interrupting her to tell the story of the little boy who cried wolf. I'm not sure it was entirely relevant to the situation, but it was the first fable that came to mind, since I didn't recall any about a little girl whose mama leaves her in Bryan, Texas, because she's being a drama queen.

Finally we got the kids back and settled at the table to eat their lunch. All was well until Honey walked in with Nena and Will. Caroline realized she had a fresh audience for her tale of woe, got up from the table, and began to hop over to where they stood while she said in her most pitiful voice, "Honey, I'm not hopping because I want to, but because I fell and scraped my knee."

Did she not learn anything from my recounting the tale of the little boy who cried wolf?

I told her to sit down and eat her nuggets before I started in on another fable, perhaps one involving children who aren't fortunate enough to spend part of their summer vacation riding the train in Waco, Texas.

After the kids finished eating lunch and got up from the table, Nena leaned over to me and whispered, "Caroline seems to enjoy ill health." Gulley mouthed to me across the table, "It takes one to know one."

Nena is herself a fan of any type of illness. In fact, if you asked her, she'd tell you she has had six surgeries in the past two years even though three of those were root canals.

Eventually we got on the road. (I wish I were kidding when I tell you I had to carry Caroline to the car because of her injury.) Everything was going smoothly until we stopped for a potty break and the kids all begged to get something to drink. Clearly we were a little off our game because we let each of them get their own twenty-four-ounce bottle of Gatorade. Then, because I am an idiot, I got in the car and made the dumbest declaration of all time.

I turned around, looked each kid in the eye, and said, "We are not making any more stops. Do not drink more than what you need to drink because there will be no more potty stops. I repeat: there will be no more potty stops. Drink only what you need."

Genius.

About five minutes later, Gulley and I were deep in conversation in the front seat when we heard some cheering and yelling coming from the backseat. We turned around to see what was going on, and I kid you not, Caroline and Will were having a Gatorade chugging contest to see who could finish their bottle first.

My first thought was that their ability to drink twenty-four ounces so quickly does not bode well for their college years. My second thought was to wonder if I needed to take Caroline to the doctor to get her hearing checked.

Sure enough, we had to stop fifteen minutes from home at a questionable truck stop so those two clowns could go to the bathroom. Rumor has it they each went for about four minutes without stopping.

When we were finally about six blocks from my house, Will announced he needed to go again. Gulley and I both said (maybe yelled), "You can hold it. It's just six blocks." I pulled up to my house and handed Gulley my house keys so she could take Will to the bathroom while I unloaded the car.

But it was too late.

Will had let himself out and was happily peeing in the yard right outside my house, which considering we were in the midst of a drought, wasn't necessarily a bad thing.

Unless you're the person in a black Suburban who drove by in time to see the whole thing.

＊

Over the years we have endured car sickness, fights over who ate more Cheetos out of the community bag, and tears because someone was belting out Jon Bon Jovi's "Livin' on a Prayer" too loudly and it hurt someone else's delicate ears. Along the way, Gulley and I have decided there is really no better indicator you're a mother than acquiring the ability to catch throw-up in a plastic bag, disinfect your hands, and immediately ask your friend to pass the beef jerky as you put on another Taylor Swift song and act as if nothing has happened. It's a unique skill set.

There have been times when we've been desperate to get home and wondered why we ever thought this was a good idea as we looked for a place to stop and take a break from the car, only to find there's not a nearby gas station or convenience store around—or a fire department where we can drop off the kids and see if they're too old to be placed for adoption.

And there have been times we've had so much fun we think we might want to buy an RV and just travel cross-country all the time. Even though I am kidding myself if I believe I could ever learn to park an RV.

But the family road trip has become a tradition. We spend all year discussing where we want to go next summer and what we'd like to see along the way. Because for us it's not about the destination as much as it is about the journey. A journey that involves stopping along the way to smell the roses or see a snake farm or drive through a Texas zoo that turns out to have only a bunch of cattle grazing in a field—as if that's exotic. And we laugh and we argue and we have moments where we could all use a time-out.

There are times when, if our drive was any indication of what Ma and Pa Ingalls went through, the Little House books should have contained the line "And then Pa kicked us out of the wagon, left us on the prairie, and said, 'Good Luck.'"

But I guarantee we'll be back on the road this summer. And every summer after that until the kids are grown and Gulley and I can finally take that trip to Cozumel.

(And I bet we'll be a little sad about it.)

(At least until they bring us our fruity drinks with the umbrellas as we lie out by the pool.)

CHAPTER 24

The Dream of the Wheaties Box

A FRIEND ONCE told me that the worst part about having children is visiting all the theme parks. I disagree. I find the theme parks fairly fun as long as the temperature is less than one hundred degrees. I think the worst part is all the extracurricular activities and the social pressure to be involved in *everything*. When did motherhood become a competitive sport?

I mean, can't I get my kid potty trained before we decide if she has what it takes to be an Olympic athlete? Or have we reached a point where we invest thousands of dollars and countless hours on gymnastics classes because we saw our toddler roll down the slide at the McDonald's PlayPlace and feel it's a sure indicator of her future athletic ability?

Don't get me wrong—I've been guilty of the same thing. Caroline learned to swim before she was two years old, and I remember many days by the pool smiling at other moms who were jamming floaties on their kids' arms while I struggled with an inordinate amount of pride, more than slightly convinced I had given birth to a child who was clearly going to be on the front of a box of Wheaties by the time she was thirteen.

There is nothing like sports and academics and every other activity to bring out some latent competitive instinct we didn't even know we had. And it doesn't help that we live in a society that thinks it's totally normal to have your child enrolled in guitar lessons and underwater macramé classes by her second birthday, lest she fall behind in her area of giftedness.

In other words, we're all crazy.

From the time I first learned I was having a baby girl, I dreamed of the day I could sign her up for ballet class and dress her in a pale-pink tutu. So as soon as she turned three years old, I signed Caroline up for a weekly ballet class. Which, soon after, became known as my weekly beating.

Oh, sure, she loved the tap shoes and the ballet slippers. She loved the leotards and the tutus. She loved watching herself in the mirror as she performed all sorts of dance moves—none of which happened to be the same routine the class was actually doing.

But because I had a deep-seated need to see my baby girl perform in a dance recital, and because I am constantly searching for ways to make my life more difficult, I signed her up to participate in the recital and wrote a check for more money than I care to admit to pay for the costume.

What I envisioned was a delicate little pink tutu with yards and yards of tulle. The reality was a hot-pink costume with glaring polka dots, complete with a huge neon-yellow bow for the top of her head. It was a costume that would cause Charo to say, "Wow. It's a little gaudy."

(Does anyone else remember when Charo used to be on *The Love Boat* almost every week? The '70s was an awesome time for inappropriate television shows that kids had no business watching.)

I barely survived that year of ballet. In fact, it's hard to talk about even now.

It's as if some latent-stage mothering tendencies rose up in me and caused me to act like an insane person. Next thing you knew, I could have found myself sitting backstage, saying, "Sweetie, put down the sippy cup and let's get this eyeliner on before we take out your hot rollers and tease your hair. And don't forget to use your sparkle fingers!"

I wept with relief when Caroline announced she was done with ballet. But after a year off, she decided to reenter the dance arena.

I supported her because that's what parents do. It's just like when my mama bought me those new roller skates with green wheels and a stopper because I had set my sights on becoming a professional roller skater. I blame the movie *Xanadu* for that ill-fated career ambition. But at least that was better than my other ambition, which involved being the best mechanical-bull rider at Gilley's and wearing white cowboy boots under my wedding dress, courtesy of *Urban Cowboy*.

When I signed Caroline up for lessons the second time around, the instructor informed me that Caroline would have to retake the class for beginners because she'd sat out for a year. Everyone knows the year you turn four is crucial for proper dance mechanics.

I was okay with it because it seemed to be dance studio policy, but on the day of her first lesson, I noticed she was about a foot taller than any of the other little girls in her class.

Also, she was one of the only ones not wearing a Huggies Pull-Up.

She thoroughly enjoyed the class the first week because she knew all the music, plus she was kind of the star of the show—if for no other reason than she didn't tee-tee in her leotard. But after the next week she told me she didn't want to be in a class with babies.

I called the dance studio and explained Caroline was the only five-year-old in a class of three-year-olds. Was there any way she could move up to the class with the other five-year-olds? They told me to show up for our scheduled class and they would evaluate her abilities to see if she could be promoted.

What exactly were we evaluating? Her ability to hold Barney in front of her while she pointed her toe out to the side? Or maybe her ability to pretend to be a fire truck as the whole class ran screaming around the room in their little ballet shoes? Or perhaps her proper use of the fake binoculars as they played the theme song from *Dora the Explorer*?

You just know that's exactly how Baryshnikov got his start.

I gently explained to the instructor that it wasn't so much about her brilliant interpretation of Dora the Explorer leaping through the rain forest as much as the fact that she knew how to go to the bathroom by herself. And with those kinds of lofty ballet goals, I knew that it was just a matter of time before she won the role of Sugarplum Fairy.

Eventually the dance teacher agreed to promote Caroline to

the five-year-old class even though she let me know she was very concerned we had fallen too far behind in our "dance career."

Our dance career?

Are you serious?

Do you think that potbellied five-year-old who picks her nose throughout the entire class is going to have a dance career just because her mama operates at a higher level of denial than I do and continues to fork out precious money for dance classes year after year? Doubtful. Whatever happened to just twirling around with your friends in a tutu that makes you feel pretty and gives your mom some nice photo ops for the family? Isn't that what dance is supposed to be?

Anyway, it all turned out to be for nothing because Caroline decided two weeks later that she wanted to quit dance once and for all. I realize some people believe you should make your kids stick with something once they've committed to it, and I agree with that, to a point. But not to the point that I was willing to subject both of us to complete misery for the next eight months. Sometimes, in the legendary words of Kenny Rogers, you got to know when to fold 'em.

And so our dance career came to an end.

✳

Later that fall, Caroline realized some of the kids in her kindergarten class were playing soccer, and she announced that if she only had one wish, that wish would be to not have a lame mom who hadn't signed her up for a soccer team. She didn't actually say that out loud, but she said it with her eyes.

I'd debated signing her up for soccer but ultimately decided that just making it to kindergarten five days a week was enough of a transition and there was no need to add a Saturday morning commitment.

When spring came, we signed up for T-ball because I realized that an inevitable part of parenthood involves spending at least thirteen years of Saturdays cheering from various sidelines. And I took comfort in knowing I'd be able to sleep in again at some point in 2021.

This was our first foray into sports, and it was okay. I enjoyed visiting with the other parents, and Caroline liked being part of a team and wearing a uniform, even though she didn't really care for T-ball because "there's too much sitting around doing nothing."

So the following fall I signed her up for soccer.

I don't know if I've ever mentioned this, but I played soccer in high school. If you want to know what that looked like, all you need to do is picture Mia Hamm. And then picture the opposite of that.

My high school had formed a brand-new girls' soccer team my senior year, and I basically made it because they'd ordered twelve uniforms and only eleven girls showed up for tryouts. The only reason I showed up in the first place was because I felt like I needed another extracurricular activity on my college applications to offset the glaring fact I'd had to take Algebra II twice.

Sadly, I spent most of the season sitting on the bench because the coach seemed to have issues with my tendency to stop running after the ball to retie the bow in my ponytail. There was also that time she tried to teach me to do a header, and I ducked and screamed. It just seems unnatural to hit a ball with your head. On purpose.

Anyway, I filled out all the registration forms for Caroline and received an e-mail letting us know they'd received our forms and our coach would be in touch to let us know about practice and whatever. But as the season drew closer and we still hadn't heard anything, I started to get a little worried. Then, finally, we got an e-mail that announced Caroline was assigned to a team but no one had volunteered to be the coach.

I think you all know how this is going to end.

Perry came home at the end of the day, and I told him the news. We agreed that we'd wait and see what happened over the weekend. Maybe someone else would volunteer. It was totally like that scene in *Footloose* where Kevin Bacon and that other guy are playing chicken with the tractors to see who would drive off the road first, except in our case there were no tractors or cool sound track involved. Yet make no mistake: we were holding out for a hero.

On Monday I e-mailed the coordinator to see if anyone had offered to coach the team (I am always the one to drive off the road first), and he responded, "No one has volunteered. We really need someone to STEP UP and coach the team." He totally threw down the all-caps STEP UP guilt gauntlet.

When Perry walked in the door later that morning, I asked, "How do you feel about us coaching soccer? Do you think we could coach?" He looked at me and said, "But neither one of us knows anything about soccer."

"I do! I played soccer in high school!"

"Like I said, neither one of us knows anything about soccer."

"Well, they're only six years old, and they don't even use a goalie. The coordinator says all we have to do is teach them to run up and down the field while kicking the ball."

Sold.

Once Perry realized it wasn't so much coaching as it was herding, he was ready to make the soccer coach commitment. I e-mailed the guy back and told him we would "STEP UP." Then I turned to Perry and said, "Oh, by the way, I'm not going to be here for the first game, so you're on your own." Sucker.

By the time we had our first practice, Perry was like a soccer coaching pro even though he refused when I asked if he wanted me to buy him some royal-blue coaching shorts and an air horn while I was at the Academy. But he did have orange cones and everything. So while his Old Navy cargo shorts didn't scream *coach*, the presence of orange cones totally made up for it.

I just knew Caroline was going to be thrilled we were coaching her team, and I couldn't wait to tell her when I picked her up from school on Monday. "Guess what?" I said. "Daddy and I are going to coach your soccer team!"

"Are y'all going to be the only coaches?"

"Yes. We're the only coaches."

"Well, that might be a little embarrassing."

Perfect. You're not even fourteen yet, kid. You don't know embarrassing.

But she changed her tune when I told her she could pick our team name, and she immediately wanted to christen us the Rainbow Unicorns. I told her that, while it was an awesome team name, it might be a little hard for our fans to cheer "Go

Rainbow Unicorns!" Rumor has it that's why more professional men's teams don't use the name.

So we became the Rainbows.

And then we were the Cheetah Girls.

And then we were the Magic.

In just one season, we had more names than Prince. But Caroline had found a sport she really enjoyed, and I tried not to let the pressure get to me when other parents started talking about academic scholarships and Olympic gold medals.

How about we teach them how to spell *cereal* before we decide it's time to put their photo on the outside of the Wheaties box?

CHAPTER 25

Adorable Cookie
Salesperson in Polyester

THE SCHOOL YEAR hadn't even started yet when I received an e-mail asking if I was interested in signing Caroline up to be part of a Brownie troop.

No. No, I am not.

But if I said that, it would be like admitting I hate puppies and boxes of fried chicken with a side of mashed potatoes. Possibly even the United States of America and democracy. Even though technically the United States is a republic. Since Caroline was only going into first grade, I wanted to remain in the category of non-ostracized society (my lack of service within the PTO already had us on the brink), so my response was vague.

(I could write an entire book on the PTO and all the ways they are masters in guilt warfare and will work you to the bone if they sense the slightest bit of weakness.)

(My best advice to you before your child enters elementary school? Learn to say no. Especially if it involves anything that ends in the words -a-thon.)

I replied, "I'm not sure if we can commit to another activity, and I certainly wouldn't have time *[or a sufficient amount of Xanax]* to lead the Brownie troop, but keep me posted and we'll see if it works out!" (I thought the exclamation point was a nice touch. It conveys that I'm excited about the possibility! Yet noncommittal!)

My strategy was twofold: if they were simply looking for some sucker to be the leader, they'd know I was nobody's patsy. And if additional messages made me suspect they might be the type of Brownie troop that would engage in questionable behaviors like camping in the actual outdoors or helping save the environment, then I'd have the heads-up to let them know our schedule was completely packed with other things and we were just sick about having to turn down the Brownies.

Time went by, school started, and I never heard another word. Just when I started to get a complex about why Caroline and I weren't good enough for Brownie Troop 3009, I received a phone call informing me we were in.

My celebration was short lived once I realized they used the phrase, "Congratulations, you're in our Brownie troop." Had there been some sort of secret Brownie rush I didn't know about? Had they checked our credentials and evaluated the sturdiness of Caroline's legs to see if she would be able to walk a mile to sell Samoas?

(And by Samoas, I mean the popular Girl Scout cookie, not the people.)

(Although now that I think about it, I believe they are referred to as Samoans. Whatever the case, they're lovely people and they also make a delicious cookie.)

There was an introductory meeting for the mothers of potential Brownies, so I decided I should attend and get a little more information about the troop. I had no idea this meeting would involve more than sipping a cup of coffee and eating a pastry but instead would require completing an enormous file folder of paperwork. Apparently being part of the Girl Scouts of America is similar to entering the CIA but with more background checks.

I sat there trying to come up with excuses for why I needed to leave, the first being my silent suffering from an extreme case of carpal tunnel syndrome, but I couldn't pull off a graceful exit. Plus, I couldn't help but think that Caroline might really enjoy being a Brownie since there was a day back in 1977 when I proudly wore the brown uniform.

And when I say "wore the brown uniform," I feel I should clarify I'm referring to my own tenure as a Brownie, not my career as a UPS driver. Not that I ever was a UPS driver, but there was a day when I wondered if I could make a living driving one of those big, brown trucks. I call that day the day I made a 13 on an exam in my intercultural communications class.

My affiliation with the Brownies lasted for only one school year. We met once a month at the neighborhood clubhouse. I looked forward to our meetings not only because we got to tie-dye shirts and paint ceramic turkeys but also because I got to carpool with my friend Jodi, and her mom drove one of those sweet wood-paneled station wagons with the seat that faced backward. That car made me face up to the deprivation of my childhood and all the unfairness that comes with having a mom who preferred to drive a Buick LeSabre, otherwise known as the Blue Sedan of No Fun, complete with Jimmy Swaggart eight-track tapes for our listening enjoyment.

To this day I can't sit on a velour seat without feeling the judgment and condemnation of passing up a tearful altar call set to piano music.

I had spent my year in Brownies making bird feeders from pinecones and making faces at the cars behind us while I rode in the back of Mrs. Jones's station wagon. Everything was fine until the day a fellow carpool member took it upon herself to inform us that there was no Santa Claus. From that day on I wanted nothing more to do with Brownies. Obviously they were all a bunch of liars because how could you doubt the validity of a man who wears a red suit and comes down your chimney once a year while he leaves his flying reindeer parked on your roof? What else would you like to tell me isn't real? The tooth fairy? Sonny and Cher's marriage? Donny Osmond's ability to see me through the TV?

But I didn't want my tainted experience to keep Caroline from being a Brownie if it was something she really wanted to do. So that night I asked, "Do you want to join a Brownie troop?"

"What are Brownies?"

"Well, it's a group of girls who wear these brown vests and do crafts and sing songs."

(And tell people that Santa Claus isn't real.)

"Okay."

How could I say no to that passionate response? I turned in all the paperwork, and we officially became part of Troop 3009.

Then I received an e-mail from the troop leader explaining we'd need to go to the Girl Scout headquarters to purchase our uniform, which is really an insult to uniforms everywhere, because since when does a brown vest made out of poly-blend constitute a uniform? What happened to the beanie and the shorts that would put you in therapy?

But I bought the vest and the numbers and a few obligatory patches that were all sold under the guise of being iron-ons because the Girl Scouts of America are shrewd and know their little troops of cookie pushers would be decimated if mothers realized they'd actually have to sew on the patches. (And, no, I didn't sew on the patches. That's what safety pins and superglue are for. How am I going to have time to pluck my eyebrows if I'm taking remedial sewing courses to show me how to sew on Brownie patches?)

One of the qualities that sold me on joining this particular Brownie troop was the promise that it would be a low-maintenance troop. We'd meet the first Friday of every month, and two mothers would take turns hosting the meeting. The first meeting went fine. It was what a Brownie meeting should be, which is to say that the girls made bracelets out of empty toilet paper rolls and ribbon, drank some Capri Suns, and had a few cookies. Perfect. Low maintenance, just as promised.

But then came the next meeting.

It was billed as a focus on promoting a healthy lifestyle. And honestly, I'm not opposed to a healthy lifestyle, as long as no one expects me to eat a carrot. What you choose to put in your digestive tract is your own personal business, so please don't judge me for my love of Mrs. Baird's Cinnamon Rolls and Tater Tots.

We arrived at the meeting, and I immediately knew I was in over my head when I saw fourteen yoga mats formed in a semicircle. And worse, upon closer inspection, I discovered they were each personally monogrammed. On every mat there were little hot-pink boxes that resembled Chinese takeout containers filled with some assortment of dried snack mix. What the actual heck? Was this a Brownie meeting or an episode of *The Martha Stewart Show*?

The mom in charge of the meeting asked the girls to sit on their yoga mats and watch while she put on a yoga demonstration. Sure, it was impressive that she could balance her entire body weight on her head, but it didn't really seem like the best move to teach to a group of impressionable, uncoordinated first graders whose parents might not want to spend a fortune in chiropractic treatments. I'm also not sure that the original yoga gurus intended for their meditative poses to be performed while listening to Miley Cyrus belt out "Party in the USA."

After the yoga demonstration was over, the host mothers filled the girls in on the importance of dental hygiene. It should have been no surprise that each girl received her very own light-up toothbrush that blinks for the amount of time you should brush your teeth. We took home more parting gifts than a contestant on *The Price Is Right*.

Actually, that's not true, because I am a master of *The Price Is Right*. All those years of watching Plinko and that little mountain climber game at Me-Ma and Pa-Pa's house totally paid off. I have no doubt that, if given the chance, I could win a new car. I'd like to believe that I could also win the Showcase Showdown, but so much of it boils down to the luck of spinning the big wheel as opposed to pure skill. And for all I know, the entire format of *The Price Is Right* is totally different now that Drew Carey has taken over. I quit watching when Bob Barker left, because he totally made that whole show. "Don't forget to spay and neuter your pets!"

At the conclusion of the dental lesson came a lecture on the dangers of smoking. It was your standard surgeon general talk: smoking is bad. It will kill you. It makes your teeth yellow. People who smoke might go to hell or, worse, drive an El Camino. The usual. But right as the discussion was winding down, I saw Caroline's hand pop up in the air. The mom in charge said, "Caroline, do you have a question?"

"No. But I just wanted to say that all my mom's cousins smoke."

(And some of them have been known to drive El Caminos.)

Perfect. Between that admission and the fact I wasn't planning to offer any monogrammed take-home items at the Brownie meeting I would eventually have to host, I felt sure we had just relegated ourselves to Troop 3653, also known as the White Trash Brownies.

But let's be honest. The Brownies weren't going to kick us out due to some smoking cousins. Sure, those other moms might have been horrified by the smoking revelation, but they needed every warm body they could get to push those cookies. Those Thin Mints don't sell themselves.

Actually, that's not true. Those cookies totally sell themselves. I think they might contain some sort of addictive substance.

Much like cigarettes.

As it turned out, we didn't get kicked out of Brownies even

though I ended up having to pay thirty-six dollars out of my own pocket because we had a cookie deficit. (I'm sure it wasn't due to any stress-eating of the Do-si-dos as we walked door to door.)

Caroline and I were on the way to our last meeting of the school year when she said, "Mama, there has got to be something more fun to do than Brownies."

Preach it, sister.

Not to mention that no one ever got a college scholarship or ended up on a box of Wheaties for their ability to paint ceramic turkeys.

We're sticking to soccer. Or swimming. Or maybe volleyball. Olympics 2020? I have a good feeling about you.

CHAPTER 26

Caroline,
the Witch, & the Wardrobe

THIS ISN'T A documented statistic, but I believe when women find out they're going to have a baby girl, at least 98 percent of them envision a wardrobe full of smocked dresses and bows. And, yes, it's heavenly to dress up your daughter like she's your own personal baby doll for the first three years of her life. Then you wake up one day and, with no warning, she suddenly has an opinion. An opinion that usually involves a plaid purple skirt with an orange-and-green-striped shirt and royal-blue knee socks.

It's a look I like to call hobo chic.

Which, frankly, is probably an insult to hobos everywhere.

I should have known I was in trouble when Caroline's pre-school teachers informed me she walked in every morning, promptly handed them the bows from her hair, and said, "No, thank you." But I was in denial and continued to buy darling outfits that actually matched for years before I finally accepted it was a lost cause.

Khalil Gibran offers these insights about children:

You may give them your love but not your thoughts,
For they have their own thoughts.
You may house their bodies but not their souls,
For their souls dwell in the house of tomorrow, which you
cannot visit, not even in your dreams.
You may strive to be like them, but seek not to make them
like you.

Yes. All of that. And I would add that you can't pick out their clothes once they decide Gap tights with a bear on the bottom aren't really the style statement they want to make.

Once Caroline began kindergarten, I discovered through a lot of trial and error that the most pain-free way to get her dressed in the morning was to offer three wardrobe options for the day. I'd walk through the kitchen on the way to the living room, holding the offerings I'd procured from her closet, and whisper to Perry, "I'm going in. Say a prayer for me." And he'd look at me as if he wanted to tell me I was the bravest woman he'd ever met. Either that or he was wondering why I was talking to him while he was looking at bargain-priced ammo online.

Most days Caroline sized up the three choices, made some editorial changes to the suggested accessories, and ultimately wore one of the outfits. But then there were the other days. The days she dismissed all my choices with a wave of her hand

and said, "None of those!" in a tone that indicated she couldn't believe I didn't have the supernatural ability to sense that she was so over leggings right now even though she loved them yesterday.

Then one day as I made my way back to the living room, holding three different outfits on hangers, the absurdity of the situation dawned on me. And it only took three years.

Suddenly I felt very much like Mary Boleyn. Except without the affair with a power-hungry king and the corsets. I had become Caroline's very own lady-in-waiting. I picked out her clothes, I fixed her hair, and I made sure she had everything she needed before she walked out the door.

And I didn't mind doing any of these things. I'm a mom. It's what I do.

But on that particular morning, as I humbly offered the three outfits carefully chosen from her closet, Caroline looked at me and said, "The problem is you and I don't have the same taste. I don't like any of these choices."

I might have become slightly unhinged. Don't mess with a woman who has just slaved over a dry bowl of Lucky Charms and cut the crusts off a ham-and-cheese sandwich.

"Well, if you don't like what I've picked out, then you can go look in your closet and choose your own outfit. It doesn't matter to me."

It was true. Yes, there was a time when I desperately wanted her to wear certain outfits with matching bows in her hair and all the right accessories. But that was before I was worn down by life and decided to settle for anything that didn't make her look like a contestant on *Toddlers & Tiaras* or a Bratz doll.

So she walked into her room, and I waited to see what she would choose. And I waited.

And I waited.

After ten minutes passed, I walked in to find her twirling around in front of her mirror. Still wearing her pajamas. And a tiara.

I was a donkey on the edge.

"Why aren't you dressed? We have to leave in two minutes!"

"I don't know what I want to wear."

I made a few more suggestions that she greeted with, "Or what else?" And I desperately wished that I could do something simpler, like broker a deal for peace in the Middle East.

Finally Perry came in to intervene and told her to put on a shirt with a pair of jeans. He might have also told me I needed to settle down. I can't remember because I had to put my head between my knees to keep from blacking out.

After the madness of the morning, I decided Mary Boleyn needed to come up with a better solution. Our mornings had become increasingly filled with wardrobe drama, and I'd even been tempted to homeschool just so we could stay in our pajamas.

When Caroline got home from school that day, I announced she was now responsible for picking out her own clothes the night before. If she forgot to do it, then she had to wear whatever I picked out, with no argument or debate about the unfairness of life and the lifelong wounds you'll suffer if your mom makes you wear a sweater dress.

A sweater dress that you begged for only two months earlier. A sweater dress that was not, in fact, woven on the devil's loom.

As it turned out, our new system wasn't much less painful

than the old system. It just took place at 6:30 p.m. instead of 7:30 a.m., and I had the comfort of knowing I could send her to bed shortly after we debated the merits of a plaid skirt versus a tie-dyed dress.

$$*$$

Which brings us to the other night. The weather forecast indicated it was going to be the coldest day of the year so far. I reminded Caroline to pick out what she wanted to wear the next day. She asked me to help her, so I obliged. I'm really not a heartless tyrant, despite my penchant for sweater dresses and clothes that match.

As we stood in her closet, she asked, "What would you wear if the weather was going to be cold and you wanted to be toasty warm?"

I pointed out a few sweater dresses and some fleece-lined tops with leggings or jeans.

She asked, "What else besides any of those things?"

Seriously. Netanyahu needs to call me. We can figure out this Middle East thing yet.

I said, "You find something. I need to go finish cooking dinner."

About three minutes later I heard her sneak into the kitchen. She threw a folded-up piece of paper at me and loudly whispered, "Open it."

I opened it.

It read, "I need help."

Don't we all, sister. Don't we all.

So, because I am a glutton for punishment, I walked back

into her room to give it another try. I showed her a few more outfits that she found unacceptable until I finally channeled my inner fashionista and asked, "What's your goal? What are you envisioning?"

"Well. I definitely want to wear my leg warmers. And two shirts. And a skirt. Maybe with some tights. And a hat."

Done.

And that is how I sent my child to school in an outfit that Punky Brewster would have envied.

The sad thing is that Caroline is only eight. When I think of how many years of this we have ahead of us, it makes me want to shell out money for a private school that requires uniforms. And we haven't even reached the age where she's conscious of name brands. I'm sure those years will be a treasure.

If memory serves, and sometimes it does, I think I was in fifth grade when it became of utmost importance for me to have Jordache jeans and Izod shirts and Nike tennis shoes. And I vividly remember in eighth grade standing in the junior department at Foley's and begging my daddy to buy me a pair of Guess overalls. Overalls that cost eighty dollars. In 1984. That's like a seven-hundred-dollar pair of pants in today's economy.

But I strongly believed those Guess overalls might change my life. They were the key to popularity and a seat at the cool lunch table. Because who could resist an awkward thirteen-year-old girl, with bangs teased beyond all reason and gravity, dressed like a farmer?

Then the other day I was getting dressed for church and realized I'd just changed into four different tops in the course of five minutes. It was with a little shock and shame that I realized Caroline comes by it naturally. Yes, it's offset by the fact that she has a father who dresses in a rotation of four Columbia fishing shirts and three pairs of khaki pants from Old Navy, but since she carries 50 percent of my DNA, I suspect she'll always have a strong propensity to be slightly obsessed with what she wears. (I once wore a leopard-print top to the zoo. When I was twenty years old. At five, that's cute. At twenty it's called overthinking your wardrobe.)

✳

It was just two mornings ago when Caroline announced that all she wanted to wear to school from now on were running shorts, leggings, and a T-shirt. I thought of all the beautiful clothes hanging in her closet—clothes she had begged me to buy—and I was furious. I threatened, "Well, I guess I'll just take all those clothes in your closet and sell them."

(Who was I going to sell them to? I've never really figured that out, but this threat has worked in the past, so I continue to use it.)

(I also feel certain there will come a day when Caroline will laugh with her friends about how her crazy mother used to threaten to sell all her clothes.)

But this time she called my bluff. "Okay," she said.

I almost couldn't see straight. It kind of ruined my whole morning.

I know. That's embarrassing.

Because what I'm finally realizing is that in spite of all my grand declarations, it's still important to me that Caroline look cute. Sure, I've surrendered in certain areas and I gave up on the bows years ago, but I worry about what other people will think when they see my child dressed like a member of the cast of *Annie* day after day.

It's my pride that wants other mothers to see Caroline walk into school and say, "Well, there goes that darling Caroline, dressed like a perfect little lady and with those darling French braids in her hair." And it's my pride that is wounded on the days I watch her walk into school and feel certain other mothers are thinking I must be out of town, because why else would my daughter's hair look like it's in the late stages of becoming dreadlocks?

But you know what? It's not about me.

There are battles along the way that are worth the fight. Like the ones that involve her safety, morality, spirituality, and general well-being. I will die on those mountains. I will fight with a vengeance, and I will nail shut bedroom windows and take away privileges and be the meanest mom in the world if that's what the situation calls for.

But clothes? Ruining every morning with a battle over what she's going to wear? In the scheme of life, it doesn't really matter. Yes, the outfit has to be appropriate and fit my parameters for no hoochies in my house, but if Caroline wants to look like she just worked out at the health club every day this year, then it's not worth the fight.

And, honestly, if you want to see some poor sartorial choices, go visit your local elementary school. The kids all look homeless. They all look like their mothers have been on extended vacations and left them at home with nothing but their color-blind fathers who don't understand hairbrush mechanics.

I have promised myself I will remember the words God spoke to Samuel before he anointed David as king of Israel: "The LORD does not look at the things people look at. People look at the outward appearance, but the LORD looks at the heart" (1 Samuel 16:7).

Maybe it's because eight years have come and gone faster than I ever could have imagined, but I've painfully started to realize that we have a pretty limited number of years to pour into our children everything we want them to know. I don't want to spend those years battling over a stupid sweater dress or braided hair, or debating whether those shorts match that shirt just because they are both pink.

I want to spend these limited years with a focus on shaping Caroline's heart, not her closet. I would say I want her to be a better version of myself, but that's not accurate. I want her to be the best version of who God has created her to be—to embrace her individual qualities and gifts. I want to teach her to put on kindness, love, gentleness, patience, and joy every morning and to walk through her day looking for ways to make a difference in her world. To be kind to the little girl in her class who struggles to fit in, to sit next to the new kid who doesn't know anyone, to stand up for the boy who gets picked on at recess. I want her to know that it's who she is inside that makes her unique and that there is no clothing available at any store that can add one ounce to her infinite worth.

Not even a pair of Guess overalls.

It's a lesson her mother still struggles with all these years later.

And even now there are days I hear myself forced to say, "You can't sleep in a Santa hat while your hair is wet and expect that it will look good the next day."

But let's be honest: that's just a life lesson every girl needs to learn.

CHAPTER 27

Little Steps of Letting Go

THE OTHER NIGHT I crawled into bed next to Caroline, and she reached out to hold my hand. As I held her warm little hand, still dimpled with the last of her baby fat, it seemed so small. Which is weird because everything about her seems so big to me lately. There have been times I've seen her from behind and almost not recognized her because there's no way that tall, gangly girl is my little baby.

But as I held her hand and watched her sleep, with her long eyelashes resting on her flawless, olive-skinned cheeks, all the petty arguments and frustrations of the day were forgotten. All the battles faded away in the fresh remembrance that she is the most perfect gift I've ever been given. That God chose to entrust this precious, hilarious, rough-and-tumble girl into my care is almost too much for me to bear.

I feel like there are so many clichés about motherhood. It's hard not to repeat what has already been said in various ways from the moment time began. And as I think about all the declarations that have been made about mother love, I realize it's because motherhood is the thing in a woman's life that catches her by total and complete surprise.

Most of us grow up with fairy tales and Barbie dolls and dreams of the day we'll meet the man we want to spend the rest of our life with. I remember watching the great romances play out before me on the movie screen—Cinderella and Prince Charming, Sandy and Danny Zuko, Bud and Sissy (because what says true love like personalized license plates in the back window of a Ford truck?)—and I hoped and prayed a day would come when I would meet a man I wanted to be with forever.

We are raised to believe we'll find our prince. Our own happily ever after. And if anything, the books and movies make it look so much easier than it really is sometimes. There are days marriage feels like throwing a wet cat and a rabid dog who leaves the toilet seat up all the time in a house together and telling them to make it work.

But then there's motherhood.

Even if we've dreamed of having babies of our own, there is nothing that prepares us for the way that moment cracks open our hearts and pours in the type of pure love we never knew existed. A love that isn't about us but is just about wanting to love and protect this little, helpless person who will emit all manner of bodily fluids on us if given half the chance. You can't fathom it until you experience it. You can decorate a nursery, scribble down baby names, and feel the miracle of a foot kicking your bladder, but none of that comes close to capturing the true moments that make a mama.

That's why I believe motherhood gives us the first true glimpse of how God loves us. The kind of love that's irrevocable, unrelenting, unconditional. I think it's the closest humans get to living out 1 Corinthians 13. Motherhood is a Holy Communion with Goldfish crackers and juice boxes.

Yet it's bittersweet. Because while we choose the person we marry with the belief and hope that it will be "till death do us part," we become mothers and immediately realize our job is to raise these little people and pour into them and pack in eighteen years of wisdom, love, and protection, only to let them go out into a world that seems scary and way too big for our comfort.

And that's where the problem lies.

We have to let them go. And from what I've seen of Caroline's childhood so far, there are little steps of letting go all along the way. Dropping her off at preschool, surrendering her to kindergarten, letting her spend the night with a friend, sending her to summer camp. The stakes get higher and higher as we send our kids out further and further.

Those walks down various school hallways are only the beginning of steps that will take them toward their own destiny. Those moments are the motherhood equivalent of riding a bike without training wheels. You just hop on and pray it all works out and the bumps and bruises are kept to a minimum. Sometimes you fall and it's a big mess, but you get right back on and continue the ride.

The irony is that the hallmark of how well we're doing our job is determined by how our children adapt to all these changes. Have we given them the security they need to function with their peers? Do they feel loved enough to pour themselves into the lives around them? Are they secure enough to jump into life with both feet and choose the daring adventure that awaits them?

And can we watch them fall and make mistakes and wrong decisions while trusting that this is all part of becoming the person God created them to be?

✳

When Caroline was about two years old, we took a trip to the beach. At some point Perry found a little crab that had lost its claws and put it in a bucket for her. She picked up that crab and carried it around like it was her baby the rest of the day. That poor crab didn't have a chance. He got loved to death from all the attention and constant handling.

I watched her with the crab as she ignored all my admonitions that the poor crab just needed to be set free if he was to have any chance of surviving. And God showed up there on that beach to teach me a lesson. Nothing survives when it's being smothered. Life, real life, requires being free to move about in the great big ocean, not being cradled in little hot hands that will stifle independence and creativity. We can't keep our crabs (or our kids) in a bucket and expect them to go far in life.

The problem is that our hearts are so intertwined with our little crabs' hearts that we don't know where theirs begin and ours end. And it's so hard to let go.

The year Caroline turned four, I was driving her to school when she announced she didn't want me to park and walk her in to school as I'd done for the last two years. Her exact words were, "Mama, drop me off by Mrs. Jane."

"Are you sure? You don't want me to walk you in?"

"Mama, I need to tell you something. You know, I'm a big girl now."

Yes. I know.

I drove through the carpool line and watched her get out of the car with her tote bag in one hand and her lunch box in the other. She walked with an extra bounce in her ponytail that made me smile as I noted the pride she felt with her new step of independence.

And then I started to cry.

You would have thought I was dropping her off at her dorm room knowing I wouldn't hear from her until she was out of money or clean clothes. Or both. I wiped my tears, told myself I was being dramatic, even for me, and wrote the whole thing off to some kind of estrogen surge.

The following Wednesday, the day before her fifth birthday, I asked her if she wanted me to walk her in or drop her off again.

Without a moment's hesitation she said, "Drop me off!"

So I did.

And I cried again.

I'd like to think it was due to PMS, but since I made it through the day without eating my body weight in M&M'S, I don't think that was the problem.

I have never been a mother who mourned all the passing signs of babyhood. Sure, I'd love to have one more day with Caroline as a newborn or a toddler, but for me, motherhood has just gotten better as I've survived breastfeeding, weaned her off the pacifier, completed our potty-training marathon, and watched the terrible threes turn into the charming fours.

But something about watching her walk into school by herself made me think of all the ways I'll have to let her go over a lifetime. The truth is, I don't want to let her go, yet I'm so proud every time I see she is self-confident enough to take these steps away from me.

I've also realized that when the day comes to drop her off at college, I might need a surplus of Kleenex and Valium. And perhaps a choir to assist me in singing "I Hope You Dance."

(Even though I'd never actually sing "I Hope You Dance." It's too much of a cliché. I'm much more likely to sing Carly Simon's "Love of My Life" or just sob silently as I drive back home while eating a chocolate donut.)

That night as I tucked Caroline into bed, I gave her a kiss and said, "Just think, that's Mama's last four-year-old kiss!"

She put her little hands on each side of my face, pulled me back down to her, kissed me softly on the cheek, and said, "That's a four-year-old kiss that you can keep forever, Mama."

And I will. I'll keep it forever.

Because raising a child is a fleeting moment in time that sometimes gets swallowed up in the daily routine of car pools and soccer practice and *Can I get away with serving tacos for dinner again tonight?* And yet it's quite possibly the most important thing we'll ever do. It's the daily balance of treasuring the moments even as we wish some of them away. It's treading water in a sea of imperfections. It's a delicate dance of guilt and joy.

At times I've thought how nice it would be if I could just

protect my daughter forever—shield her from hurt feelings, a broken heart, dreams that may not come true. But I realize all those things in my own life have been part of making me who I am today. Had I been protected from all the unpleasant moments life can bring, I wouldn't have learned who I really am. Caroline's character will have to be built and shaped by the joys and heartaches she will face over her lifetime.

I have to say it's a little frightening. And a lot gut wrenching.

✳

For Caroline's eighth birthday she decided she wanted to get her ears pierced. We went to the mall, even though I had no idea if she'd actually go through with it or not. My doubts only grew stronger when she asked if we could just look at clothes for a while instead. But eventually we made our way to Claire's, and she looked at the various starter earring options and weighed the decision as carefully as I've ever seen her think about anything. Then she spotted a pair of sparkly green earrings that seemed to erase all her doubts.

Ultimately the desire for those earrings outweighed her fears. I told the salesgirl we were ready to proceed with the piercing. And so she began to mark Caroline's ears.

I've never seen a person look more solemn or nervous.

And I felt like my own heart was about to jump out of my chest. I knew exactly what she was feeling, and I wanted to protect her from the fear and help her conquer it all at the same time. About two seconds later, they squeezed the triggers, and she officially had pierced ears.

She let out a loud gasp. I held my breath, not sure if she was going to cry or scream or completely freak out. And then she said, "That didn't hurt at all!" I'm not sure if that was totally true, but I think her complete giddiness over her new, sparkly green earrings trumped any pain. She jumped on me and hugged me, so full of joy and excitement. And my heart almost couldn't take it.

I told her a million times how proud I was of her for facing her fears and tried to turn it into a life lesson about how sometimes the anticipation of a thing is worse than the actual event. But honestly, I think that's a lesson she already knows. She approaches life with a kind of fearlessness I've never known.

My prayer for her is that she will be like those sparkly green earrings she chose at the mall that day. Shiny, happy, and colorful, with a blinding glimmer every time they catch the light. When she entered our lives, it turned our black-and-white world into a place filled with unimaginable color and sparkle. Daniel 12:3 says that those who are wise will "shine like the brightness of the heavens, and those who lead many to righteousness, like the stars for ever and ever."

I want her to catch the light of Jesus Christ and never let go.

Last Mother's Day one of our worship leaders was the guest speaker. She talked about motherhood, and one thing she said has stuck with me: "When we loosen our grip, he tightens his."

I know I've made some mistakes with Caroline, and I'm sure I'll make more, but he doesn't make mistakes. He loves unconditionally. His plans and purposes are perfect. He created her with a purpose and a plan for this time, for this generation.

My job is to strive to lead her to him in everything I do. To show her that even though there are times I can't be there and times (like from the ages of twelve to eighteen) she'll act like she doesn't necessarily want me there, God is always there. Watching, catching, loving, and molding her into the person she was created to be. She's safer in his grip than she'll ever be in mine.

He has created more personality in my girl's little body than a human being should be allowed. I can't wait to see what he does with it.

Even if there are times I'll need to cry a little bit in my car.

While eating a chocolate donut.

Mothering Caroline is the greatest joy I've ever known. The most important thing I'll ever do. And I love her more than she'll ever know.

At least until she has a child of her own.

Acknowledgments

I CAN'T EVEN pretend that this book would have happened without the support and love of the following people. I mean, I could pretend, but it would be a lie. And if I'm going to start lying, I'll start with my weight or my age.

Perry: Part of the reason I finally sat down and wrote this book is because you never quit asking, "When are you going to write that book?" Yes, it got on my nerves, but I love you for it. You help me find the laughter in everything. There's no one I'd rather share this life with.

Dad and Cherrie: I hope this makes you feel like you've gotten some kind of return on the investment you made in my college education, since I know my grades didn't accomplish that. I love you both so much. Thanks for always seeing the best in me and for teaching me to love with my whole heart. There are few things I love more than watching the way Caroline lights up when her Mimi and Bops walk into the room.

Gulley: Thank you for convincing me that if *Paul Blart: Mall Cop* could be the number one movie in America, then there was a market for this book, because that movie was a clear sign that we live in a world where people are desperate for a reason to laugh. You have always believed in me, and you've saved me hundreds of thousands of dollars in therapy. I love you more than my luggage.

Amy: I'm so glad you are my sister. I never would have showered during Caroline's first year of life if you hadn't been such a great aunt. I love you.

Honey and Big: I'm thankful that you took me in and allowed me to stay and eat your food and sleep in your beds all these years.

Sophie: I'm so glad we met on the Internet. And I'm still amazed that it happened to two introverts who sometimes pretend to be extroverts. Thank you for all the encouragement and for listening to me talk all those years about "the book" I was going to write "someday."

Jennifer Clouse: You are the bravest person I know. And I can't thank you enough for putting on your consultant hat when I was trying to figure out cover art. I love you.

Birthday Club: Y'all are my sanity. Thanks for being so excited for me. Here's to many more years of monthly Mexican food together.

Bill: I knew the first time I met you that our paths would cross again. I'm thankful that I finally sent that e-mail to the right address. You are the best agent I could ever hope for and the only reason I was ever able to figure out how to write a book proposal.

Stephanie: You have made this book better than it ever would have been without you. I love having you as my editor. And I love saying, "I have an editor." It sounds very professional.

Lisa Jackson and the Tyndale team: I am grateful to all of you for taking a chance on me. I knew Tyndale was the right choice, but I had no idea how right until I met you all in person and knew I'd found my people.

My blog readers: The encouragement and support y'all have given me over the years overwhelm me. Thank you for showing up every day to read what I write.

And, most of all, God: I am humbled by your love for me and by the mercy and grace you continue to pour out on this undeserving soul.

About the Author

MELANIE SHANKLE was in fourth grade when her teacher asked her to read aloud a story she had written to the entire class. Even though that story now seems a little silly and simplistic, it made the students in Mrs. Rice's homeroom laugh out loud, and a little dream began in Melanie's heart—a dream to use words to make people laugh.

Over the ensuing years, Melanie wrote when she had a chance and tucked things away in notebooks and journals, rarely showing any of it to anyone. But in July 2005, on a total whim and in desperate need of a creative outlet, she began writing a blog called Big Mama. No one was more shocked than Melanie when someone other than her dad and her college roommate began to read it.

Since that time Melanie has seen her blog readership grow beyond her wildest dreams and open the doors to writing and speaking opportunities she never could have imagined. It's proof that God wasn't playing around when he inspired Paul to write Ephesians 3:20. It is "immeasurably more" than she could have asked or imagined.

In addition to her blog, Melanie writes a quarterly column for the popular online magazine *Praise and Coffee*, is a regular contributor to the Pioneer Woman's blog, and serves as co-administrator and writer for LifeWay Women's AllAccess blog. She also serves as emcee for LifeWay's annual DotMom event and participates in Compassion International's blogger initiative.

A graduate of Texas A&M University and a former pharmaceutical rep, Melanie loves writing, shopping at Target, looking to see what's on sale at Anthropologie, and encouraging other moms in a humorous yet relatable way at theBigMamaBlog.com.

Most of all, she loves being the mother of Caroline and the wife of her husband, Perry. The three of them live in San Antonio, Texas, with their two elderly dogs. She also believes she owes a debt of gratitude to Mrs. Rice for making her read that story out loud all those years ago.

a little SALTY to cut the sweet

Southern Stories
of Faith,
Family, and
Fifteen Pounds
of Bacon

SOPHIE HUDSON
author of BooMama blog

Coming summer 2013!

I love M_____ ha___ _____ _____ _____ o_
many _____ th_
pages. _____ _____ly insightful, witty, relatable, wide ope_
passionate about Jesus. She likes people, and I like that in a
In this book, Melanie lives her life with us and invites us to
lives with her. Relish this ride, sister! You won't be sorry you

BETH MOORE
New York Times bestselling author and Bible study teacher

In her memoir, Melanie uses an irresistible combination of
the-corner-of-your-eye emotion and laugh-so-loud-you-scar
the-cat humor. Every chapter of *Sparkly Green Earrings*—ac
every page—is a splendid journey through sudden, side-spli
laughter and utterly relatable tears . . . and back to laughter
She captures every fear, crazy notion, nervous breakdown, a
desperate moment of new motherhood so expertly and hila
that I actually wondered if she'd tapped into my memory of
my first child. And all throughout the book, as Caroline grc
and starts school (and has a very short stint in Brownies), M
establishes just how much her faith has guided and propelle
through this miraculous privilege known as motherhood. H
memoir is nothing short of a delight.

REE DRUMMOND
New York Times bestselling author of *The Pioneer Woman Cooks*

What happens when you read a book that's one part *Blue Like Jazz*,
one part Anita Renfroe, and two parts Big Mama? You laugh too
loud, nod till your neck hurts, and throw your hands up with a
relieved *yes*! Simply put: I love Melanie Shankle, and every page of
this book shimmers with her fabulous voice, honest hilarity, and
the light of a Savior that makes even the wackiest, hardest days of
motherhood somehow glimmer with something grand. *Sparkly
Green Earrings*—the perfect accessory to be dazzled by grace and
more than a glint of God.

ANN VOSKAMP
New York Times bestselling author of the *One Thousand Gifts*

Melanie's writing is insightful, hilarious, and full of encouragement for the journey. *Sparkly Green Earrings* is refreshment for the soul. For all the reasons thousands of people love her blog, you will be smitten with her book. Mostly because you will fall in love with Melanie through its pages, and more important, with the God she serves.

KELLY MINTER
Bible study author, writer, and speaker

Melanie has the rare gift of making you embarrass yourself laughing while considering the deeper undertones of each story. I don't know a mama who would say that parenting is exactly what she thought it would be all the time. It's a delicate dance we do, this balancing of the ordinary and the holy, and often we get it wrong. The ability to pull the humanity out and examine it in the wake of what really matters is not an easy task, but it's one Melanie has done exquisitely. As writers, we pray our words string together in a way that connects our flesh to the Storyteller, and I'm so honored to have my endorsement on a book that does that as well as this one does. I dare you to read it without laughing, without seeing your own life embedded in its corners. You're in for a journey with a beautiful woman who, in my estimation, has a lot more light catching to do around a million more turns. Her wit, humility, and true writing ability will make you want to chase her as she goes.

ANGIE SMITH
Author of *I Will Carry You* and *What Women Fear*